C++

PROGRAMMING FOR GAME DEVELOPMENT

"Mastering C++ for Building Fast, Reliable, and Engaging Games for PC and Consoles"

MICHAEL A. CHAMPAGNE

Table of Contents

Part I:

Foundations of C++ for Game Development

CHAPTER 1

Introduction to C++ in Game Development

This chapter lays the foundation for understanding why C++ is the language of choice for many professional game development studios. It explores the inherent strengths of C++, the unique demands of game development, and the essential steps to setting up a robust development environment.

1.1 The Power of C++ in Game Engines

C++ has been a cornerstone of game development for decades, and its enduring relevance stems from a potent combination of features:[1]

- Performance:

- Games are inherently performance-critical applications.[2] Real-time rendering, complex physics simulations, and intricate AI calculations demand raw speed. C++ allows for direct memory manipulation and low-level control, enabling developers to squeeze every ounce of performance from the hardware.[3]
- Its compiled nature translates to efficient machine code, minimizing overhead and maximizing execution speed. This is crucial for maintaining smooth frame rates and responsive gameplay.
- C++ allows for optimization at the instruction level, which is a key advantage.[4]

- Control:

- C++ grants developers granular control over system resources, including memory, CPU, and GPU.[5] This level of control is essential for managing complex game engines and optimizing performance.
- It facilitates direct interaction with hardware, enabling developers to implement custom rendering pipelines, physics engines, and other core game systems.[6]

- Flexibility:
  - C++ is a multi-paradigm language, supporting procedural, object-oriented, and generic programming.[7] This flexibility allows developers to choose the[8] most appropriate approach for different game components.
  - It's highly portable, allowing games to be developed for a wide

range of platforms, including PC, consoles, and mobile devices.[9]

- C++ is the base language for many game engines such as Unreal Engine.[10]

- Mature Ecosystem:
  - C++ has a rich and extensive standard library, providing a wealth of tools and functionalities.[11]
  - A vast ecosystem of third-party libraries and frameworks is available, simplifying complex tasks like graphics rendering, physics simulation, and audio processing.
  - The community is very large, and therefore finding solutions to problems is often easier.

1.2 Understanding Performance-Critical Applications

Game development is a unique domain where performance is paramount. Here's why:

- Real-Time Rendering:
    - Games require rendering complex 3D scenes at high frame rates (e.g., 60 FPS or higher) to create smooth and immersive experiences.
    - This involves processing millions of polygons, applying complex shaders, and managing large textures, all within a fraction of a second.
- Physics Simulations:
    - Realistic physics simulations, such as collisions, gravity, and fluid dynamics, demand significant computational power.[12]

- Accurate and responsive physics are essential for creating believable and engaging gameplay.
- Artificial Intelligence (AI):
  - AI-driven characters and behaviors require complex algorithms for pathfinding, decision-making, and interaction.[13]
  - Efficient AI implementations are crucial for creating challenging and engaging gameplay experiences.
- Input Handling:
  - Games must react to player input with minimal latency.
  - Input handling must be very efficient to provide a feeling of responsiveness.
- Resource Management:
  - Games frequently handle large amounts of data, like textures,

audio files, and level information.

○ Efficient memory management is essential to avoid crashes and slowdowns.[14]

1.3 Setting Up Your Development Environment (Visual Studio, Xcode, GCC)

A well-configured development environment is crucial for efficient game development. Here's a breakdown of common options:

- Visual Studio (Windows):
    ○ A powerful and comprehensive IDE (Integrated Development Environment) widely used for Windows game development.[15]
    ○ Provides excellent debugging tools, code editing features, and integration with Microsoft's DirectX graphics API.

- ○ Visual studio is very well optimized for C++ development.[16]
- ○ Can be used with other compilers.
- Xcode (macOS):
  - ○ Apple's IDE for macOS and iOS development, essential for creating games for Apple platforms.
  - ○ Offers seamless integration with Apple's Metal graphics API and provides robust debugging and profiling tools.[17]
  - ○ Xcode is the standard IDE for mac and IOS development.[18]
- GCC (Cross-Platform):
  - ○ The GNU Compiler Collection, a versatile and open-source compiler that supports multiple platforms.[19]
  - ○ Often used in conjunction with other tools and IDEs, such as CMake and makefiles.

- Very portable, and can be used on many different operating systems.
- Can be integrated into many IDEs.
- Essential Tools:
  - Compiler: Translates C++ code into machine code.
  - Debugger: Helps identify and fix errors in code.
  - IDE: Provides a user-friendly interface for coding, debugging, and project management.[20]
  - Version Control (Git): Tracks changes to code and facilitates collaboration.[21]

1.4 Project Structure and Organization for Games

A well-organized project structure is essential for managing large and complex game projects. Here are some key considerations:

- Separation of Concerns:

- Divide the project into logical modules, such as rendering, physics, audio, and AI.
- This promotes code reusability and maintainability.
- Asset Management:
  - Organize game assets (textures, models, audio files) in a consistent and hierarchical manner.
  - Use a robust asset management system to load and manage assets efficiently.
- Code Organization:
  - Use clear and consistent naming conventions for variables, functions, and classes.
  - Follow established coding standards to ensure code readability and maintainability.
  - Utilize namespaces, and folders to organize code.
- Build System:

- Use a build system (e.g., CMake, Make, or Visual Studio solutions) to automate the compilation and linking process.
- This simplifies the build process and ensures consistency across different platforms.

- Documentation:
  - Comment your code.
  - Document the design and architecture of the game.
  - Document the usage of all custom made functions.
- Version Control:
  - Use version control to track changes to the code base.
  - This is very important for collaboration, and for backing up your work.

By mastering these foundational concepts, you'll be well-equipped to embark on your journey into C++ game development.

CHAPTER 2

C++ Fundamentals Revisited: Essential Concepts for Games

This chapter reinforces core C++ concepts with a focus on their application and optimization within the context of game development. We'll explore data types, variables, operators, and control flow, emphasizing performance and clarity.

2.1 Data Types, Variables, and Operators (Optimized Usage)

In game development, efficiency is paramount. The choice of data types and operators can significantly impact performance.

- Data Types:
    - Integer Types (int, short, long, long long, uint32_t, etc.):

- Understanding the size and range of different integer types is crucial. In games, where memory usage is often critical, using the smallest appropriate integer type can save memory and improve cache locality.
- uint32_t and similar fixed-width integer types are often preferred for cross-platform compatibility and predictable behavior.
- Bitwise operations are frequently used for manipulating flags and masks, which are essential for managing game states and rendering options.
  - Floating-Point Types (float, double):

- float is typically preferred over double for most game calculations due to its lower memory footprint and faster computation. However, double might be necessary for scenarios requiring high precision, such as large-scale simulations or physics calculations.
- Floating-point operations can be computationally expensive.[1] Optimizing these calculations is vital for maintaining smooth frame rates.
- Consider the usage of fixed point math when applicable.
  - Boolean Type (bool):
    - Efficiently managing boolean flags is crucial for game logic. Using bitfields

or packed booleans can optimize memory usage when dealing with numerous boolean states.

- Character Types (char, wchar_t):
  - Character types are used for text and string manipulation.[2] Optimizing string operations is essential for UI rendering and text-based game elements.
  - Consider the encoding of characters, especially for internationalization.

- Variables:
  - Scope and Lifetime:
    - Understanding variable scope (local, global, static) and lifetime is crucial for memory management and avoiding unintended side effects.[3]

- Minimize the scope of variables to improve code clarity and reduce the risk of naming conflicts.
- Avoid unnecessary global variables, as they can lead to tight coupling and make code harder to maintain.
- Initialization:
    - Always initialize variables before using them to prevent undefined behavior.
    - Use constructor initialization lists for class members to ensure proper initialization.
- Memory Alignment:
    - Understanding memory alignment is important for optimizing data access. Misaligned data can lead to performance penalties.[4]

- Use the alignas keyword when necessary.
- Operators:
  - Arithmetic Operators (+, -, *, /):
    - Optimize arithmetic operations by minimizing unnecessary calculations and using efficient algorithms.
    - Consider using lookup tables or precomputed values for frequently used calculations.
  - Bitwise Operators (&, |, ^, ~, <<, >>):
    - Bitwise operators are powerful tools for manipulating flags, masks, and bit patterns.[5]
    - They are often used for optimizing game states, rendering options, and network communication.

- Comparison Operators (==, !=, <, >, <=, >=):
    - Optimize comparison operations by minimizing unnecessary comparisons and using early exits.
    - Consider using the ternary operator for simple if/else statements.
- Increment and Decrement Operators (++, --):
    - Understand the difference between prefix and postfix increment/decrement operators.
    - Prefix operators are generally more efficient when the return value is not used.

2.2 Control Flow: Branching and Looping for Game Logic

Control flow statements are the backbone of game logic. Optimizing these statements is crucial for performance and responsiveness.

- Branching (if, else, switch):
  - If-Else Statements:
    - Optimize if-else statements by arranging conditions in order of likelihood.
    - Minimize the number of nested if-else statements to improve code readability and performance.
  - Switch Statements:
    - Switch statements are often more efficient than long chains of if-else statements, especially when dealing with discrete values.[6]

- Use switch statements for state machines and other scenarios where multiple conditions need to be checked.
  - Ternary Operator (?:):
    - Use the ternary operator for concise and efficient conditional expressions.
    - This operator can improve code readability and reduce the number of lines of code.
- Looping (for, while, do-while):
  - For Loops:
    - Optimize for loops by minimizing the number of iterations and avoiding unnecessary calculations within the loop.
    - Use loop unrolling or other techniques to improve performance when dealing

with small, fixed-size
loops.
- While Loops:
  - Use while loops for
    scenarios where the
    number of iterations is
    unknown.
  - Ensure that while loops
    have a termination
    condition to prevent
    infinite loops.
- Do-While Loops:
  - Similar to while loops, but
    the code block is executed
    at least once.[7]
- Loop Optimizations:
  - Loop Invariant Code
    Motion: Move calculations
    that don't depend on the
    loop variable outside the
    loop.[8]
  - Loop Unrolling: Replicate
    the loop body multiple

times to reduce loop overhead.

- Vectorization: Utilize SIMD instructions to perform operations on multiple data elements in parallel.[9]
- Cache Locality: Arrange data and loop iterations to maximize cache hits.

By understanding and applying these optimized C++ fundamentals, you can build efficient and responsive game systems that deliver a smooth and engaging player experience.

2.3 Functions, Scope, and Parameter Passing (Performance Considerations)

Functions are the building blocks of modular and reusable code.[1] However, their implementation and usage can significantly impact performance.[2]

- Functions:

- Function Overhead:
  - Function calls incur overhead due to stack frame setup, parameter passing, and return value handling.[3] In performance-critical sections of code, minimizing function calls is essential.
  - Consider using inline functions for small, frequently called functions to eliminate function call overhead.[4]
- Function Pointers and Function Objects:
  - Function pointers and function objects (functors) provide flexibility but can introduce overhead.
  - Use function pointers or functors judiciously, especially in

performance-sensitive areas.

- Lambda functions are very useful, and can be used in many situations.

- Recursion:
  - Recursion can be elegant but can lead to stack overflow and performance issues.[5]
  - Prefer iterative solutions over recursive ones whenever possible, especially for deeply recursive algorithms.
- Const correctness:
  - Using the const keyword wherever possible, makes the code safer, and can allow the compiler to make optimizations.[6]

- Scope:
  - Local Scope:

- Minimize the scope of variables to improve code clarity and reduce the risk of naming conflicts.
- Declare variables as close to their usage as possible.
- Global Scope:
    - Avoid excessive use of global variables, as they can lead to tight coupling and make code harder to maintain.[7]
    - Use namespaces to organize global variables and prevent naming collisions.[8]
- Static Scope:
    - Static variables within functions retain their values between function calls.[9]
    - Use static variables judiciously, as they can introduce statefulness and

make code harder to reason about.

- Parameter Passing:
  - Pass by Value:
    - Passing parameters by value creates a copy, which can be expensive for large objects.[10]
    - Avoid passing large objects by value unless necessary.
  - Pass by Reference:
    - Passing parameters by reference avoids copying, improving performance.[11]
    - Use pass-by-reference for large objects or when modifying the original object is required.
  - Pass by Const Reference:
    - Passing parameters by const reference avoids copying and prevents accidental modification of the original object.[12]

- Use
  pass-by-const-reference
  for large objects that
  should not be modified.
  - Return Values:
    - Returning large objects by
      value can be expensive.[13]
    - Consider using return
      value optimization (RVO)
      or move semantics to
      minimize copying.

2.4 Memory Management: Stack vs. Heap (Dynamic Allocation in Games)

Efficient memory management is critical for game performance and stability.[14]

- Stack Memory:
  - Automatic Allocation:
    - Stack memory is
      automatically allocated
      and deallocated for local

variables and function call frames.[15]

- Stack allocation is fast and efficient.[16]

- Limited Size:
  - The stack has a limited size, which can lead to stack overflow if excessive memory is allocated.
  - Avoid allocating large objects on the stack.

- Scope and Lifetime:
  - Stack variables have a limited scope and lifetime, determined by the function or block in which they are declared.[17]
  - Stack memory is automatically reclaimed when the function or block exits.[18]

- Heap Memory (Dynamic Allocation):
  - Manual Allocation:

- Heap memory is manually allocated and deallocated using new and delete (or new[] and delete[]).
- Heap allocation is slower than stack allocation.[19]

○ Flexible Size:
  - The heap provides a large pool of memory, allowing for dynamic allocation of objects of varying sizes.[20]
  - Heap memory can be allocated and deallocated at runtime.[21]

○ Memory Leaks:
  - Failure to deallocate heap memory can lead to memory leaks, which can degrade performance and cause crashes.[22]
  - Use smart pointers or other resource management techniques to prevent memory leaks.

- Fragmentation:
    - Repeated allocation and deallocation of heap memory can lead to fragmentation, which can reduce performance.[23]
    - Use memory pools or custom allocators to minimize fragmentation.[24]
- Allocation patterns:
    - Understanding the patterns of allocation and deallocation of your game is very important.
    - Allocating many small objects can cause fragmentation.
    - Allocating and deallocating in real time can cause stutters.
- Smart pointers:
    - Smart pointers like unique_ptr, and shared_ptr, are very useful

for managing heap allocated objects, and reducing memory leaks.[25]

- ○ Custom allocators:
  - ■ For games requiring very high performance, custom allocators are often used.[26] These allocators can be optimized for the specific needs of the game.

By mastering these concepts, you'll be able to write efficient and robust C++ code that optimizes performance and minimizes memory-related issues in your game development projects.

CHAPTER 3

Object-Oriented Programming (OOP) in Game Design

OOP provides a structured and modular approach to game development, enabling developers to create flexible, maintainable, and scalable game systems.[1]

3.1 Classes and Objects: Representing Game Entities

At the heart of OOP are classes and objects, which allow developers to model real-world entities and game concepts in a natural and intuitive way.[2]

- Classes:
  - A class is a blueprint or template that defines the properties (data members) and behaviors (member functions) of an object.[3]

- o In game development, classes can represent various entities, such as players, enemies, items, environments, and UI elements.[4]
- o Classes promote code reusability by encapsulating related data and functionality.[5]
- o Classes help in creating a logical structure of the game.
- Objects:
  - o An object is an instance of a class, a concrete realization of the blueprint.[6]
  - o Each object has its own unique state, represented by the values of its data members.[7]
  - o Objects interact with each other by invoking member functions, enabling complex game behaviors.
  - o Objects are the runtime representation of the game's elements.
  - o Representing Game Entities:

- Player Class:
  - Data members: position, health, inventory, score.
  - Member functions: move(), attack(), takeDamage(), interact().
- Enemy Class:
  - Data members: position, health, attack power, AI state.
  - Member functions: move(), attack(), takeDamage(), updateAI().
- Item Class:
  - Data members: position, type, properties.
  - Member functions: use(), pickup(), drop().

- Environment Class:
    - Data members: terrain, objects, lighting.
    - Member functions: render(), update(), interact().

3.2 Encapsulation, Inheritance, and Polymorphism: Building Flexible Systems

These three core OOP principles are essential for creating robust and adaptable game architectures.

- Encapsulation:
    - Encapsulation involves bundling data and functions that operate on that data within a single unit (class).[8]
    - It[9] controls access to data by using access specifiers (public, private, protected), preventing

unintended modifications and ensuring data integrity.[10]

- Encapsulation promotes modularity and information hiding, making code easier to maintain and modify.[11]
- Encapsulation allows for the creation of interfaces, that are used to interact with the object.[12]

- Inheritance:
  - Inheritance allows creating new classes (derived classes) that inherit properties and behaviors from existing classes (base classes).[13]
  - It promotes code reuse and reduces redundancy by allowing derived classes to inherit common functionality from base classes.[14]
  - Inheritance establishes an "is-a" relationship between classes (e.g., a "Dog" is-a "Animal").

- In game development, inheritance allows for the creation of hierarchies of game objects.[15] Example.
    - Base Class: Character (common properties and behaviors for all characters).
    - Derived Classes: Player, Enemy, NPC (specific properties and behaviors for each character type).
  -

- Polymorphism:
  - Polymorphism allows objects of different classes to be treated as objects of a common base class.[16]
  - It enables dynamic binding, where the appropriate[17] function is called at runtime based on the object's actual type.
  - Polymorphism promotes flexibility and extensibility by allowing new classes to be added

without modifying existing code.[18]

- ○ Polymorphism is often implemented using virtual functions and abstract classes.
- ○ Example:
  - Base Class: GameObject (virtual function render()).
  - Derived Classes: Player, Enemy, Item (override render() to implement specific rendering logic).
  - A collection of GameObject pointers can be rendered without knowing the specific type of each object.
- ○ Polymorphism allows for the creation of systems that can handle many different types of objects, in a very elegant way.[19]
- Benefits in Game Development:

- Modularity: OOP breaks down complex game systems into smaller, manageable modules.[20]
- Reusability: Inheritance and composition enable code reuse, reducing development time and effort.[21]
- Maintainability: Encapsulation and modularity make code easier to understand, modify, and debug.[22]
- Extensibility: Polymorphism allows for adding new game features and content without modifying existing code.[23]
- Flexibility: OOP enables the creation of adaptable and dynamic game systems that can handle a wide range of scenarios.
- Organization: OOP helps in organizing the complex game code, into logical and manageable parts.[24]

By mastering these OOP principles, game developers can create well-structured, maintainable, and scalable game systems that deliver engaging and immersive experiences.

3.3 Abstract Classes and Interfaces: Designing Game Components

These tools are essential for defining robust and flexible game component architectures.

- Abstract Classes:
  - An abstract class is a class that cannot be instantiated.[1] It serves as a base class for other classes.
  - It defines a common interface for its derived classes, specifying the methods that derived classes must implement.
  - Abstract classes can contain both abstract methods (pure virtual functions) and concrete methods.[2]

- Abstract classes define "what" derived classes must do, but not "how."
- In game development, abstract classes are used to represent generic concepts or behaviors.[3]
  - Example: An Actor abstract class could define common methods like update() and render(), which are then implemented by specific actor types like Player and Enemy.
-
- Abstract classes enforce a consistent structure across related classes.[4]
- Use Cases:
  - Defining a base for a group of related objects.
  - Forcing derived classes to implement certain functions.

- ■ Creating base classes that define an interface.
- Interfaces:
  - An interface is a purely abstract class that contains only pure virtual functions (no data members or concrete methods).
  - It defines a contract that classes must adhere to, specifying the methods that implementing classes must provide.[5]
  - Interfaces allow for multiple inheritance, enabling a class to implement multiple interfaces.[6]
  - In C++, interfaces are often implemented using abstract classes with only pure virtual functions.[7]
  - Interfaces promote loose coupling and enable polymorphism, allowing objects of different classes to be treated interchangeably.[8]
  - Use Cases:

- Defining a contract for a specific behavior.
- Allowing objects of different types to be treated uniformly.
- Enabling multiple inheritance.
- Creating pluggable systems.
  - Differences:
    - Abstract classes can have data members and concrete methods, interfaces cannot.
    - Abstract classes define a base class with some implementation, interfaces define a contract with no implementation.
    - Abstract classes are used for "is-a" relationships, interfaces are used for "can-do" relationships.
- Designing Game Components:

- Use abstract classes and interfaces to define clear and consistent interfaces for game components.
- This promotes modularity, reusability, and maintainability.
- Example: An IDrawable interface could define a draw() method, which is then implemented by all drawable game objects.
- This allows a rendering system to treat all drawable objects uniformly.

3.4 Design Patterns: Applying OOP Principles to Game Architecture

Design patterns are reusable solutions to common software design problems.[9] They provide a vocabulary and framework for building robust and maintainable game architectures.

- Common Game Development Design Patterns:
  - Singleton:
    - Ensures that a class has only one instance and provides a global point of access to it.
    - Used for managing global resources like game managers, input handlers, and audio systems.
  - Factory:
    - Creates objects without specifying the exact class of object that will be created.
    - Used for creating game objects dynamically, based on game data or user input.
  - Observer:
    - Defines a one-to-many dependency between objects, so that when one

object changes state, all its dependents are notified and[10] updated automatically.

- Used for[11] event systems, UI updates, and game state management.

○ State:

- Allows an object to alter its behavior when its internal state changes.
- Used for implementing AI behaviors, animation systems, and game state machines.

○ Command:

- Encapsulates a request as an object, allowing for parameterization of clients with queues, requests, and operations.[1213]
- Used for input handling, undo/redo systems, and scripting.

- Component:
  - Allows you to compose object functionality by attaching components at runtime.
  - Very popular in game engine design, it allows for very flexible game object creation.
- Object Pool:
  - Maintains a pool of pre-allocated objects, avoiding the overhead of creating and destroying objects frequently.
  - Used for optimizing performance in games that create and destroy many objects.[14]
- Benefits of Using Design Patterns:
  - Code Reusability: Design patterns provide reusable solutions to common problems.[15]

- Code Maintainability: Patterns promote well-structured and organized code.[16]
- Code Extensibility: Patterns make it easier to add new features and modify existing code.[17]
- Improved Communication: Design patterns provide a common vocabulary for discussing design solutions.[18]
- Reduced Development Time: Patterns provide proven solutions, reducing the need to reinvent the wheel.

- Applying Design Patterns in Game Architecture:
  - Identify common design problems in your game and apply appropriate design patterns.
  - Use design patterns to create modular, flexible, and maintainable game systems.[19]

- Document your design decisions and explain the rationale behind using specific patterns.
- Proper use of design patterns, can greatly improve the quality, and maintainability of game code.[20]

By mastering abstract classes, interfaces, and design patterns, game developers can create robust, scalable, and maintainable game architectures that support complex and engaging gameplay experiences.

CHAPTER 4

Advanced C++ Concepts for Game Performance

This chapter delves into advanced C++ techniques that are essential for building high-performance and robust game systems.

4.1 Templates and Generic Programming: Creating Reusable Components

Templates and generic programming are powerful tools for creating reusable and efficient code.[1]

- Templates:
  - Templates allow you to write code that can work with different data types without duplicating code.[2]
  - They enable the creation of generic classes and functions

that can be instantiated with specific types at compile time.[3]

- Templates enhance code reusability and reduce code duplication, promoting maintainability and reducing errors.[4]
- In game development, templates are used for creating generic data structures, algorithms, and utility functions.
- Template Specialization:
    - Allows you to provide specific implementations of templates for certain data types.
    - This is useful for optimizing performance or handling special cases.
- Use Cases:
    - Creating generic containers (e.g., vectors, lists, maps).

- Implementing generic algorithms (e.g., sorting, searching).
- Creating generic math libraries (e.g., vectors, matrices).
- Creating reusable game component systems.

- Generic Programming:
  - Generic programming focuses on writing code that is independent of specific data types.[5]
  - It promotes code reusability and flexibility by separating algorithms from data structures.[6]
  - Generic programming allows for creating highly optimized and efficient code.
  - Concepts:
    - Concepts are a feature introduced in C++20 that allows you to define

requirements for template parameters.[7]

- They improve type safety and provide more informative error messages.

- Benefits in Game Development:
  - Code Reusability: Templates enable the creation of reusable components that can be used across different game systems.
  - Performance: Templates are resolved at compile time, eliminating runtime overhead.[8]
  - Type Safety: Templates provide compile-time type checking, reducing the risk of runtime errors.[9]
  - Flexibility: Templates allow for creating highly adaptable and

configurable game systems.[10]

- Reduced code duplication: Generic programming minimizes code duplication, making code more maintainable.[11]

4.2 Smart Pointers and Resource Management: Avoiding Memory Leaks

Smart pointers and proper resource management are crucial for preventing memory leaks and ensuring robust game systems.[12]

- Smart Pointers:
  - Smart pointers are objects that manage the lifetime of dynamically allocated memory.[13]
  - They automatically deallocate memory when it is no longer needed, preventing memory leaks.

- C++ provides several smart pointer types:[14]
    - std::unique_ptr: Represents exclusive ownership of a dynamically allocated object.[15]
        - The object is automatically deleted when the unique_ptr goes out of scope.
        - unique_ptr cannot be copied, but it can be moved.
    - ■
    - std::shared_ptr: Represents shared ownership of a dynamically allocated object.[16]
        - The object is deleted when the last shared_ptr pointing

to it goes out of scope.

- shared_ptr uses reference counting to track the number of owners.

■

- std::weak_ptr: A non-owning smart pointer that provides access to an object managed by a shared_ptr.
  - weak_ptr does not affect the object's lifetime.
  - It can be used to prevent circular dependencies between shared_ptr objects.

○

○ Benefits in Game Development:
  - Memory Safety: Smart pointers eliminate the risk

of memory leaks and dangling pointers.[17]

- Resource Management: Smart pointers can manage other resources besides memory, such as file handles and network connections.[18]
- Exception Safety: Smart pointers automatically release resources when exceptions are thrown.[19]
- Simplified Code: Smart pointers simplify memory management, making code cleaner and easier to maintain.[20]

- Resource Management:
  - Resource management involves ensuring that resources (memory, files, network connections) are properly acquired and released.[21]

- RAII (Resource Acquisition Is Initialization) is a C++ idiom that ties the lifetime of a resource to the lifetime of an object.[22]
- RAII ensures that resources are automatically released when the object goes out of scope.
- Best Practices:
  - Use smart pointers to manage dynamically allocated memory.
  - Use RAII to manage other resources.
  - Avoid manual memory management whenever possible.
  - Use try/catch blocks to handle exceptions and ensure that resources are released.
  - Create resource managers, to handle the loading, and unloading of game assets.

- Memory Pools:
  - A memory pool is a technique for allocating and deallocating memory in fixed-size blocks.[23]
  - Memory pools can improve performance by reducing memory fragmentation and allocation overhead.[24]
  - They are often used for allocating frequently created and destroyed objects, such as particles or projectiles.
- Custom Allocators:
  - For very high performance games, custom allocators can be implemented.[25]
  - Custom allocators can be optimized for the specific memory allocation patterns of a game.[26]

By mastering templates, generic programming, smart pointers, and resource management, game developers can create high-performance, robust, and maintainable game systems that deliver exceptional player experiences.

4.3 Move Semantics and Rvalue References: Optimizing Data Transfer

Move semantics and rvalue references are crucial for optimizing data transfer and reducing unnecessary copying in game development.[1]

- Rvalue References:
    - An rvalue reference is a reference that binds to a temporary object (rvalue).[2]
    - Rvalue references are denoted by &&.
    - They allow you to distinguish between lvalues (objects with persistent storage) and rvalues (temporary objects).
    - Rvalue references are essential for implementing move semantics.

- Move Semantics:
  - Move semantics allow you to transfer ownership of resources from a temporary object to another object without copying the data.[3]
  - This is achieved by "moving" the resources rather than copying them.
  - Move semantics are particularly beneficial for large objects, such as textures, meshes, and audio buffers, where copying can be expensive.[4]
  - Move operations are implemented using move constructors and move assignment operators.[5]
  - Move Constructors and Move Assignment Operators:
    - These special member functions are called when an object is constructed or assigned from an rvalue.[6]

- They "steal" the resources from the rvalue, leaving it in a valid but unspecified state.
- This avoids unnecessary deep copies, improving performance.
- std::move():
  - The std::move() function casts an lvalue to an rvalue, allowing you to move its resources.
  - However, std::move() does not actually move anything; it simply enables the move operation.
- Benefits in Game Development:
  - Performance Optimization: Move semantics significantly reduce copying overhead, especially for large objects.[7]

- Resource Management: Move semantics enable efficient resource transfer, reducing memory allocations and deallocations.[8]
- Simplified Code: Move semantics can simplify code by eliminating the need for manual copying.
- Improved efficiency: By avoiding unneeded copies, games can run much smoother.

- Perfect Forwarding:
  - Perfect forwarding allows you to forward function arguments to other functions without losing their value category (lvalue or rvalue).
  - This is achieved using template parameter deduction and std::forward().

- Perfect forwarding is essential for creating generic functions that can handle both lvalues and rvalues.

4.4 Lambda Expressions and Function Objects: Simplifying Event Handling

Lambda expressions and function objects provide concise and flexible ways to handle events and callbacks in game development.

- Lambda Expressions:
  - Lambda expressions are anonymous functions that can be defined inline.
  - They provide a concise syntax for creating function objects.
  - Lambda expressions can capture variables from their enclosing scope, allowing them to access and modify local variables.[9]
  - They are often used for event handlers, callbacks, and other

situations where small, self-contained functions are needed.

- ○ Capture Clauses:
  - ■ Capture clauses specify how variables from the enclosing scope are captured by the lambda expression.[10]
  - ■ []: Captures nothing.
  - ■ [&]: Captures all variables by reference.
  - ■ [=]: Captures all variables by value.
  - ■ [x, &y]: Captures x by value and y by reference.
- ○ Benefits in Game Development:
  - ■ Concise Syntax: Lambda expressions simplify code by eliminating the need to define separate function objects.
  - ■ Flexibility: Lambda expressions can capture

variables from their enclosing scope, providing access to local data.[11]

- Readability: Lambda expressions can improve code readability by keeping event handlers and callbacks close to where they are used.
- Event Handling: They are useful for creating inline event handlers.

- Function Objects (Functors):
  - Function objects are objects that can be called like functions.[12]
  - They are implemented by overloading the operator().
  - Function objects can store state, allowing them to maintain data between function calls.
  - They are more flexible than function pointers, as they can store data and implement custom behavior.[13]

- std::function:
  - The std::function class template provides a generic way to store and invoke callable objects, including function pointers, function objects, and lambda expressions.
  - It allows you to store different types of callable objects in a uniform way.
- Benefits in Game Development:
  - Stateful Callbacks: Function objects can store state, enabling them to maintain data between callbacks.
  - Custom Behavior: Function objects can implement custom behavior, providing greater flexibility than function pointers.[14]

- Generic Callbacks: std::function allows you to create generic callback systems that can handle different types of callable objects.
- Event systems: They allow for very flexible event systems.

By mastering move semantics, rvalue references, lambda expressions, and function objects, game developers can create highly optimized, flexible, and maintainable game systems that deliver exceptional performance and player experiences.

Part II:

Game Engine Architecture and Core Systems

CHAPTER 5

Building a Game Loop and Time Management

This chapter focuses on the fundamental structure of a game and how to manage time effectively to ensure a consistent and enjoyable player experience.

5.1 Understanding the Game Loop: Update, Render, Input

The game loop is the heart of any interactive game. It's a continuous cycle that processes player input, updates the game state, and renders the graphics.[1]

- The Game Loop Structure:
  - The basic structure of a game loop involves three primary phases:[2]
    - Input Handling:

- This phase gathers and processes player input from various devices (keyboard, mouse, gamepad).
- It translates raw input into game-specific actions.
- Efficient input handling is crucial for responsiveness.[3]
- Update:
  - This phase updates the game state based on player input and game logic.[4]
  - It involves simulating physics, updating AI, managing game logic, and handling collisions.[5]

- The update phase is where the game's core logic resides.
  - Render:
    - This phase draws the game's graphics to the screen.[6]
    - It involves rendering 2D or 3D scenes, drawing UI elements, and applying visual effects.
    - The render phase is responsible for visually representing the game state.[7]
  -
  - Loop Execution:
    - These three phases are executed repeatedly in a continuous loop.
    - The loop continues until the player quits the game.[8]

- The frequency of the loop's execution is the frame rate (frames per second, FPS).
  - Example Pseudocode:

C++

```
while (gameIsRunning) {
  handleInput();
  updateGameState();
  renderGraphics();
}
```

- Importance of Each Phase:
  - Input Handling:
    - Ensures that the game responds to player actions in a timely manner.
    - Provides a sense of control and immersion.
  - Update:
    - Determines the game's behavior and progression.
    - Simulates the game world and manages its dynamics.
  - Render:

- Creates the visual experience for the player.
- Conveys information and enhances immersion.
  ○ Loop Management:
  - The game loop must be managed effectively to prevent the game from freezing or running too fast.
  - Techniques such as capping the frame rate or using delta time are used to stabilize the game loop.[9]

5.2 Fixed vs. Variable Time Steps: Ensuring Smooth Gameplay

Time management is critical for creating consistent and smooth gameplay. Two primary approaches are used: fixed and variable time steps.

- Variable Time Steps:

- Concept:
  - The update phase is executed based on the actual time elapsed since the last frame (delta time).
  - Delta time is calculated by measuring the time between frames.[10]
  - This approach allows the game to run smoothly even if the frame rate fluctuates.
- Advantages:
  - Smooth gameplay on systems with varying performance.
  - No need to cap the frame rate.
- Disadvantages:
  - Inconsistent physics simulations if the frame rate varies significantly.
  - Potential for gameplay inconsistencies if the

update logic is not carefully designed.

- o Implementation:

C++
```
while (gameIsRunning) {
    float deltaTime = calculateDeltaTime();
    handleInput();
    updateGameState(deltaTime);
    renderGraphics();
}
```

- Fixed Time Steps:
  - o Concept:
    - ■ The update phase is executed at a fixed time interval, regardless of the actual frame rate.[11]
    - ■ If the frame rate is lower than the fixed update rate, multiple update steps are performed per frame.
    - ■ This approach ensures consistent physics simulations and gameplay.

- Advantages:
    - Consistent physics simulations and gameplay.
    - Deterministic behavior.
- Disadvantages:
    - Potential for jerky movement if the frame rate is significantly lower than the fixed update rate.
    - Requires careful management of the update loop to avoid performance issues.
- Implementation:

C++

```cpp
const float fixedTimeStep = 1.0f / 60.0f; // 60 updates per second
float accumulator = 0.0f;

while (gameIsRunning) {
    float deltaTime = calculateDeltaTime();
    accumulator += deltaTime;

    handleInput();
```

```
while (accumulator >= fixedTimeStep) {
    updateGameState(fixedTimeStep);
    accumulator -= fixedTimeStep;
}

renderGraphics();
}
```

- Choosing the Right Approach:
    - Variable time steps are generally preferred for games where visual smoothness is paramount, and physics accuracy is less critical.
    - Fixed time steps are essential for games with complex physics simulations or multiplayer games where consistency is crucial.
    - Hybrid approaches can also be used, where physics are updated with a fixed time step and other game logic is updated with a variable time step.

- Delta Time Considerations:
  - It is very important to use delta time in all movement, and physics calculations, when using variable time steps.
  - This will allow for the game to run at different framerates, while maintaining the same game speed.

By understanding and implementing effective game loop and time management techniques, game developers can create smooth, responsive, and enjoyable gameplay experiences that adapt to varying hardware capabilities.

5.3 High-Resolution Timers and Performance Profiling

Accurate timing and performance profiling are essential for optimizing game performance and identifying bottlenecks.[1]

- High-Resolution Timers:

- Necessity:
    - Standard system timers often lack the precision required for accurate frame timing and performance measurement.
    - High-resolution timers provide sub-millisecond accuracy, enabling precise measurement of frame durations and code execution times.[2]
- Platform-Specific Implementations:
    - Windows: QueryPerformanceCounter() and QueryPerformanceFrequency() provide access to high-resolution timers.
    - Linux/macOS: std::chrono::high_resolution_clock or

clock_gettime() with CLOCK_MONOTONIC provide high-resolution timing capabilities.

- Usage:
  - High-resolution timers are used to calculate delta time, measure frame durations, and profile code execution times.
  - They are essential for accurate performance analysis and optimization.
- Example (C++):

C++

```
#include <chrono>

auto startTime = std::chrono::high_resolution_clock::now();
// Code to be timed
auto endTime = std::chrono::high_resolution_clock::now();
std::chrono::duration<double> duration = endTime - startTime;
```

```
double elapsedTime = duration.count();
```

- Performance Profiling:
  - Purpose:
    - Performance profiling involves measuring and analyzing the execution time of different parts of the game code.
    - It helps identify performance bottlenecks and areas for optimization.[3]
  - Techniques:
    - Instrumentation: Inserting timing code at strategic points in the code to measure execution times.
    - Profiling Tools: Using specialized profiling tools (e.g., Intel VTune, AMD Radeon GPU Profiler, or built in profilers in IDEs)

to collect and analyze performance data.[4]

- Sampling: Periodically sampling the program counter to determine which functions are consuming the most CPU time.

○ Data Analysis:

- Analyzing profiling data to identify performance bottlenecks and areas for optimization.[5]

- Visualizing profiling data using graphs and charts to gain insights into performance trends.

○ Importance:

- Profiling is essential for identifying and resolving performance issues.[6]

- It enables developers to optimize code and improve game performance.

- Profiling should be done on the target hardware.
  - Common Bottlenecks:
    - CPU bound operations.
    - GPU bound operations.
    - Memory bandwidth limitations.
    - Disk IO.

5.4 Delta Time and Frame Rate Independence

Delta time and frame rate independence are crucial for creating smooth and consistent gameplay experiences across different hardware configurations.[7]

- Delta Time:
  - Definition:
    - Delta time is the time elapsed between two consecutive frames.[8]
    - It is used to normalize game updates and ensure that game logic runs

consistently regardless of the frame rate.[9]
- o Calculation:
  - Delta time is calculated by measuring the time between the start of the current frame and the start of the previous frame.[10]
- o Usage:
  - Delta time is used to scale game updates, such as movement, physics simulations, and animation.[11]
  - It ensures that game logic runs at the same speed regardless of the frame rate.[12]
- o Example (C++):

C++

```
float deltaTime = calculateDeltaTime();
position += velocity * deltaTime;
```

- Frame Rate Independence:

- Goal:
  - Frame rate independence aims to create gameplay experiences that are consistent across different hardware configurations and frame rates.[13]
- Importance:
  - It ensures that players have a consistent gameplay experience regardless of their hardware.
  - It prevents gameplay inconsistencies caused by varying frame rates.
- Implementation:
  - Using delta time to scale game updates.
  - Implementing fixed time steps for critical game logic.

- Using smooth interpolation techniques to hide frame rate variations.
  - Benefits:
    - Consistent gameplay across different hardware.
    - Smoother gameplay experiences.
    - Reduced reliance on specific hardware configurations.
  - Interpolation:
    - Interpolation is used to smooth out the rendering of objects, when using fixed time steps, but variable rendering.
    - This helps to reduce visual judder.

By mastering high-resolution timers, performance profiling, delta time, and frame rate independence, game developers can create high-performance, consistent, and enjoyable gameplay experiences that adapt to a wide range of hardware configurations.

CHAPTER 6

Input Handling and Event Management

This chapter focuses on the crucial aspects of capturing player input and managing events within a game, ensuring responsive and intuitive gameplay.

6.1 Keyboard, Mouse, and Gamepad Input: Cross-Platform Considerations

Handling input across various platforms (PC, consoles, mobile) requires careful consideration of device differences and platform-specific APIs.[1]

- Keyboard Input:
  - Challenges:
    - Keycodes can vary across platforms and keyboard layouts.[2]

- Handling modifier keys (Shift, Ctrl, Alt) requires careful management.
- Key repeat behavior can differ between operating systems.
- Cross-Platform Strategies:
  - Use an abstraction layer to map platform-specific keycodes to a consistent set of game-defined actions.
  - Provide configurable key bindings to allow players to customize controls.
  - Implement consistent key repeat behavior across platforms.
- Example:
  - Create an enum or a set of defines that are used to represent game actions.
  - Create a class that maps the operating system

keycodes to the game
actions.

- Mouse Input:
  - Challenges:
    - Mouse input can vary in
      sensitivity and precision
      across different devices
      and operating systems.[3]
    - Handling relative vs.
      absolute mouse movement
      requires different
      approaches.
    - Mouse button mappings
      can differ.
  - Cross-Platform Strategies:
    - Provide options for
      adjusting mouse
      sensitivity and
      acceleration.
    - Implement consistent
      mouse button mappings
      across platforms.
    - Use relative mouse
      movement for camera

control and absolute mouse movement for UI interaction.

- Example:
  - Provide options for inverting the mouse y axis.
  - Provide a sensitivity slider.
- Gamepad Input:
  - Challenges:
    - Gamepad layouts and button mappings can vary significantly across different controllers (Xbox, PlayStation, Nintendo).
    - Handling analog stick input and trigger values requires careful calibration.
    - Gamepad support can vary across operating systems.
  - Cross-Platform Strategies:
    - Use a gamepad API or library that provides a

consistent interface across different controllers. SDL2, and GLFW are examples.
- Implement configurable gamepad bindings to allow players to customize controls.
- Provide options for calibrating analog stick and trigger inputs.
  - Example:
    - Provide dead zone options for analog sticks.
    - Provide rumble feedback support.
- Cross-Platform Considerations:
  - Abstraction Layers:
    - Use abstraction layers to encapsulate platform-specific input APIs and provide a consistent interface to the game logic.

- This allows the game to be ported to different platforms without modifying the core input handling code.
  - Input Mapping:
    - Implement flexible input mapping systems that allow players to customize controls.
    - This improves accessibility and caters to different player preferences.
  - Device Detection:
    - Implement robust device detection mechanisms to identify and handle different input devices.
    - This ensures that the game can handle a wide range of input devices.
  - Input Buffering:

- Implementing input buffers, is very important for reducing input lag.

6.2 Event Systems: Implementing Custom Events and Callbacks

Event systems are essential for decoupling game logic and enabling flexible communication between game components.[4]

- Event System Concepts:
  - Events:
    - Events represent occurrences or actions within the game (e.g., player death, item pickup, UI button click).
    - Events can carry data related to the occurrence.[5]
  - Event Listeners:
    - Event listeners are objects or functions that subscribe

to events and are notified when they occur.[6]
- Listeners can perform actions in response to events.[7]
  - Event Dispatcher:
    - The event dispatcher manages the registration and notification of event listeners.
    - It receives events and distributes them to the appropriate listeners.
- Implementing Custom Events:
  - Event Classes:
    - Define event classes to represent specific types of events.
    - Event classes can contain data related to the event.[8]
  - Event Listeners:
    - Implement event listener interfaces or function objects to handle events.

- Listeners can perform actions in response to events.[9]
  - Event Dispatcher:
    - Create an event dispatcher class to manage event registration and notification.
    - The dispatcher can use a map or other data structure to store event listeners.
- Callbacks:
  - Function Pointers and Function Objects:
    - Callbacks are functions or function objects that are invoked when an event occurs.[10]
    - They provide a flexible way to handle events and decouple game logic.
  - Lambda Expressions:

- Lambda expressions provide a concise way to define inline callbacks.[11]
- They are often used for simple event handlers.
  - std::function:
    - The std::function class template provides a generic way to store and invoke callable objects.
    - It allows you to store different types of callbacks in a uniform way.
- Benefits of Event Systems:
  - Decoupling: Event systems decouple game components, making code more modular and maintainable.[12]
  - Flexibility: Event systems allow for dynamic and flexible communication between game components.[13]
  - Extensibility: Event systems make it easy to add new event

types and listeners without modifying existing code.
- ○ Modularity: event systems promote modular design.[14]
- ○ Maintainability: Code is easier to maintain.
- Considerations:
  - ○ Event Queues:
    - ■ Use event queues to handle events asynchronously and prevent race conditions.[15]
    - ■ This is particularly important for handling input events and network events.
  - ○ Event Filtering:
    - ■ Implement event filtering mechanisms to allow listeners to subscribe to specific types of events.
    - ■ This improves efficiency and reduces unnecessary event notifications.

- Event Prioritization:
  - Implement event prioritization, to handle important events first.

By implementing robust input handling and event management systems, game developers can create responsive, intuitive, and engaging gameplay experiences that adapt to a wide range of input devices and platforms.

6.3 Input Buffering and Debouncing: Handling User Input Effectively

These techniques are essential for smoothing out input inconsistencies and preventing unintended input triggers.

- Input Buffering:
  - Purpose:
    - Input buffering involves storing input events in a queue or buffer before processing them.[1]

- This helps to smooth out input inconsistencies and prevent input loss due to frame rate variations or system lag.
- Benefits:
  - Reduced Input Lag: Buffering can reduce the perceived input lag by processing input events asynchronously.[2]
  - Smoother Input Handling: Buffering can smooth out input inconsistencies and prevent jittery movement.[3]
  - Handling Input Spikes: Buffering can handle sudden bursts of input events, such as rapid mouse clicks or keyboard presses.
- Implementation:

- Use a queue or circular buffer to store input events.
- Process input events from the buffer at a consistent rate, independent of the frame rate.
- Consider implementing a maximum buffer size to prevent memory exhaustion.
  - Example:
    - Create a queue that stores input events with timestamps.
    - Process the queue in the update loop, using the timestamps to interpolate input values.
    - This is especially useful for fighting games, or any game that requires precise timing.[4]
- Debouncing:

- Purpose:
  - Debouncing involves filtering out spurious input events caused by mechanical switch bounce or other noise.
  - This is particularly important for handling button presses and other discrete input events.
- Benefits:
  - Preventing Double Triggers: Debouncing prevents unintended double triggers of button presses.
  - Smoothing Out Input: Debouncing smooths out input signals and prevents jittery input.[5]
  - Improved Input Accuracy: Debouncing improves the accuracy of input handling.[6]

- Implementation:
  - Use a timer or state machine to track the time since the last input event.
  - Ignore input events that occur within a short time interval after the previous event.
  - Adjust the debouncing interval based on the input device and the game's requirements.
- Example:
  - When a button is pressed, start a timer.
  - Ignore any subsequent button presses until the timer expires.
  - This technique is very important for hardware that has mechanical switches.

6.4 Input Mapping and Configuration: Customizing Controls

Providing players with the ability to customize controls is essential for accessibility and player preferences.

- Input Mapping:
  - Purpose:
    - Input mapping involves associating game actions with specific input devices and controls.
    - This allows players to customize their control schemes and use different input devices.
  - Benefits:
    - Improved Accessibility: Input mapping allows players with disabilities to customize controls to suit their needs.[7]

- Player Preferences: Input mapping allows players to customize controls to their personal preferences.
- Support for Different Input Devices: Input mapping allows the game to support a wide range of input devices.[8]
- Implementation:
  - Use a configuration file or in-game menu to allow players to customize controls.
  - Provide options for mapping keyboard keys, mouse buttons, gamepad buttons, and other input devices.
  - Allow players to create and save multiple control profiles.
- Example:

- Create a configuration file that stores input mappings as key-value pairs.
- Provide an in-game menu that allows players to select and modify input mappings.
- Allow players to save and load custom control profiles.
- Input Configuration:
  - Purpose:
    - Input configuration involves providing players with options for adjusting input settings, such as sensitivity, acceleration, and dead zones.
    - This allows players to fine-tune their input devices for optimal performance.
  - Benefits:

- Improved Precision: Input configuration allows players to fine-tune their input devices for optimal precision.
- Reduced Input Lag: Input configuration can reduce input lag by optimizing input settings.[9]
- Enhanced Player Experience: Input configuration enhances the overall player experience by providing greater control over input devices.
  - Implementation:
    - Provide options for adjusting mouse sensitivity, acceleration, and dead zones.
    - Provide options for calibrating gamepad analog sticks and triggers.

- ■ Allow players to save and load custom input configurations.
  - ○ Example:
    - ■ Provide sliders for adjusting mouse sensitivity and acceleration.
    - ■ Provide options for setting dead zones for gamepad analog sticks.
    - ■ Allow players to save and load custom input configurations.
- • Considerations:
  - ○ User-Friendly Interface:
    - ■ Design a user-friendly interface for input mapping and configuration.
    - ■ Provide clear and concise instructions for customizing controls.
  - ○ Default Control Schemes:

- Provide sensible default control schemes for different input devices.
- This ensures that players can start playing the game without having to configure controls.
  - Platform-Specific Considerations:
    - Consider platform-specific input conventions and best practices.
    - This ensures that the game feels natural and intuitive on different platforms.
  - Accessibility:
    - Always consider accessibility when designing input systems.
    - Allow for full remapping, and provide options for players with disabilities.

By mastering input buffering, debouncing, input mapping, and configuration, game developers can create highly polished and user-friendly input systems that enhance the player experience and cater to a wide range of player preferences and abilities.

CHAPTER 7

Graphics Programming with C++

API Design Philosophies and Trade-offs:
- OpenGL's Abstraction:
  - Historically, OpenGL aimed for a higher level of abstraction, shielding developers from the raw hardware.[1]
  - This abstraction simplified initial development but could lead to performance bottlenecks due to driver overhead.
  - OpenGL's state-machine design, while conceptually simple, can become complex to manage in large applications.[2]
- DirectX's Hardware Proximity:

- DirectX, particularly Direct3D, has always prioritized close-to-the-metal access, allowing developers to exploit the full potential of Windows-based hardware.[3]
- This direct control translates to high performance but requires a deeper understanding of the underlying hardware.
  - Vulkan's Explicit Control:
    - Vulkan takes this low-level approach to the extreme, giving developers explicit control over nearly every aspect of the GPU.[4]
    - This explicit control minimizes driver overhead and enables highly optimized rendering pipelines.[5]

- However, the increased control comes at the cost of increased complexity and boilerplate code.
  o API Layering and Abstraction:
    - Game engines and middleware often introduce abstraction layers to bridge the differences between graphics APIs.[6]
    - These layers provide a unified interface, simplifying cross-platform development and allowing developers to focus on game logic rather than API specifics.[7]
    - However, abstraction layers can introduce their own performance overhead, so careful design and optimization are essential.[8]

- The Future of Graphics APIs:
  - Graphics APIs continue to evolve, with features like ray tracing, mesh shaders, and variable-rate shading becoming increasingly common.[9]
  - Understanding the underlying principles of graphics programming remains essential, even as APIs become more sophisticated.

7.2 Shader Programming: Introduction to GLSL/HLSL

- Shader Execution Model and Parallelism:
  - SIMD Architecture:
    - GPUs employ a Single Instruction, Multiple Data (SIMD) architecture, executing the same shader

code on many pixels or vertices simultaneously.[10]

- Understanding SIMD parallelism is crucial for optimizing shader performance.

○ Warp/Wavefront Execution:

- GPUs group threads into warps (NVIDIA) or wavefronts (AMD), which execute in lockstep.[11]

- Branching within a warp can lead to performance penalties, as threads may diverge and execute different code paths.[12]

○ Shader Optimization Techniques:

- Minimize Branching: Use conditional expressions (ternary operator) or predication to avoid branching.

- Vectorization: Use vector operations to take advantage of SIMD parallelism.[13]
- Reduce Texture Lookups: Texture lookups are expensive; minimize them whenever possible.
- Optimize Arithmetic Operations: Use low-precision floating-point types (mediump, lowp) when possible.
- Use Precomputed Values: Precompute constants and lookup tables to reduce runtime calculations.
- Avoiding Divergent Control Flow: structure code to minimize control flow changes within a warp or wavefront.
- Shader Debugging and Profiling:

- Debugging Challenges:
  - Debugging shaders can be challenging due to the parallel nature of GPU execution and the lack of traditional debugging tools.[14]
- Debugging Tools:
  - RenderDoc provides powerful debugging and profiling capabilities for graphics APIs.[15]
  - Graphics debuggers integrated into IDEs can help identify shader errors.[16]
- Profiling Techniques:
  - GPU profiling tools can identify performance bottlenecks in shaders.[17]

- Frame analysis tools can help visualize shader execution and identify areas for optimization.[18]
  - Advanced Shader Techniques:
    - Compute Shaders for GPGPU:
      - Compute shaders enable general-purpose GPU computing, allowing developers to perform tasks like physics simulations, image processing, and AI on the GPU.[19]
    - Ray Tracing Shaders:
      - Ray tracing shaders enable realistic lighting and reflections by simulating the path of light rays.[20]

- Mesh Shaders:
    - Mesh shaders provide more control over geometry processing, allowing for advanced mesh manipulation and generation.[21]
    - Variable Rate Shading (VRS):
        - VRS allows for varying the shading rate across different regions of the screen, improving performance without significantly impacting visual quality.[22]
- SPIR-V and Cross-API Shaders:
    - SPIR-V is an intermediate representation for shaders, allowing for cross-API shader compilation.[23]

- Tools like glslangValidator and dxc can compile GLSL and HLSL to SPIR-V.[24]
- This enables greater portability of shader code across different graphics APIs.
- Shader Libraries and Frameworks:
  - Libraries and frameworks can simplify shader development by providing reusable shader code and utility functions.[25]
  - Examples include:
    - GLM (OpenGL Mathematics): A header-only library for vector and matrix operations.[26]
    - Dear ImGui: A library for creating immediate-mode

user interfaces with
shaders.[27]

By understanding the intricacies of graphics
APIs and mastering the art of shader
programming, game developers can create
visually stunning and performant games
that push the boundaries of real-time
graphics.

7.3 Rendering Techniques: 2D and 3D Graphics Basics

2D Rendering Techniques:

- Sprite Batching and Optimization:
    - Sprite batching involves rendering multiple sprites in a single draw call, reducing CPU overhead and improving performance.[1]
    - Techniques like sorting sprites by texture or shader state can further optimize batching.[2]

- Using index buffers for sprite quads can reduce vertex buffer size.
- Parallax Scrolling:
    - Parallax scrolling creates a sense of depth by moving background layers at different speeds.[3]
    - This technique is commonly used in 2D platformers and side-scrolling games.[4]
- Render Textures and Off-Screen Rendering:
    - Render textures allow rendering 2D graphics to an off-screen buffer, which can then be used as a texture for other rendering operations.
    - This technique is useful for creating dynamic effects like reflections, shadows, and post-processing.[5]

- UI Rendering and Scalable Vector Graphics (SVG):
    - UI rendering requires efficient handling of text, images, and interactive elements.[6]
    - Scalable Vector Graphics (SVG) can be used to render resolution-independent UI elements.[7]
    - Libraries like FreeType and stb_truetype can be used for text rendering.[8]
- 2D Lighting and Shadows:
    - Although 2D games, are typically less lighting intensive than 3D games, lighting and shadows can add depth and atmosphere.[9]
    - Techniques like normal mapping and shadow

mapping can be adapted for 2D rendering.[10]

- Pixel Art and Retro Rendering:
  - Pixel art games often require specific rendering techniques, such as nearest-neighbor filtering and integer scaling.[11]
  - Retro rendering effects, like scanlines and dithering, can be used to emulate classic game consoles.

- 3D Rendering Techniques (Continued):
  - Advanced Lighting Models:
    - Physically Based Rendering (PBR) models simulate realistic lighting and material properties, creating more immersive scenes.[12]
    - Global illumination techniques, like ray tracing

and screen-space ambient occlusion (SSAO), enhance realism.[13]

- Geometry Instancing:
  - Geometry instancing allows rendering multiple instances of the same mesh with different transformations and material properties.[14]
  - This technique is efficient for rendering large numbers of identical objects, such as trees, rocks, and particles.
- Particle Systems:
  - Particle systems simulate dynamic effects like fire, smoke, and explosions.[15]
  - Techniques like GPU particle systems and compute shaders can be used to optimize particle rendering.[16]

- Terrain Rendering:
  - Terrain rendering involves generating and rendering large, detailed landscapes.[17]
  - Techniques like heightmaps, tiled terrain, and procedural generation are used to create realistic terrain.
- Animation Techniques:
  - Skeletal animation and morph target animation are used to animate 3D characters and objects.[18]
  - Animation blending and interpolation techniques create smooth and realistic animations.
- Post-Processing Effects:
  - Post-processing effects, like bloom, depth of field, and motion blur, enhance

the visual quality of the rendered scene.[19]

- These effects are typically implemented using framebuffers and shaders.
- Ray Tracing and Path Tracing:
  - Real time raytracing, and path tracing are becoming more and more common in modern games.
  - These techniques allow for very realistic lighting effects.

7.4 Resource Management: Textures, Meshes, and Materials, Advanced Texture Management:

- Texture Compression:
  - Texture compression techniques, like S3TC and ASTC, reduce texture memory usage without significant loss of quality.

- Choosing the appropriate compression format is crucial for balancing quality and performance.
- Texture Streaming and Mipmap Generation:
  - Texture streaming loads textures asynchronously, preventing stalls during gameplay.[20]
  - Mipmap generation creates progressively smaller versions of textures, improving rendering performance and reducing aliasing.
- Texture Atlases and Array Textures:
  - Texture atlases combine multiple textures into a single texture, reducing draw calls and improving performance.[21]

- Array textures store multiple textures in a single array, enabling efficient texture switching.
  - Virtual Texturing:
    - Virtual texturing allows for the rendering of extremely large textures, by only loading the visible portions of the texture.[22]
- Advanced Mesh Management:
  - Mesh Optimization Techniques:
    - Vertex compression, index buffer optimization, and mesh simplification reduce mesh memory usage and improve rendering performance.[23]
    - Level of detail (LOD) techniques render meshes with varying levels of detail based on their distance from the camera.[24]

- Procedural Mesh Generation:
  - Procedural mesh generation creates meshes dynamically, reducing the need for pre-authored assets.[25]
  - This technique is useful for creating dynamic environments and effects.
- Geometry Shaders and Tessellation:
  - Geometry shaders and tessellation allow for dynamic mesh manipulation and generation on the GPU.[26]
  - These techniques can be used to create complex geometry and effects.
- Advanced Material Management:
  - Material Instancing:
    - Material instancing allows rendering multiple objects

with the same material but different parameters.[27]

- This technique reduces draw calls and improves performance.

- Shader Variants and Uber Shaders:
    - Shader variants allow creating multiple versions of a shader with different features and optimizations.[28]
    - Uber shaders combine multiple shader variations into a single shader, reducing shader switching overhead.

- Material Pipelines:
    - Creating material pipelines, allows for the creation of complex material effects, by combining multiple shaders.

- Resource Caching and Pooling:
    - Resource caching, and resource pooling, are both very important for reducing the amount of time required to load in game assets.[29]

By mastering these advanced rendering techniques and resource management strategies, game developers can create visually stunning and performant games that push the boundaries of real-time graphics.

CHAPTER 8

Game Physics and Collision Detection

This chapter explores the essential techniques for simulating realistic physics and detecting collisions in game environments.

8.1 Implementing Basic Physics Simulations (Movement, Gravity)

Simulating basic physics phenomena like movement and gravity is crucial for creating believable and engaging gameplay.[1]

- Movement:
  - Velocity and Acceleration:
    - Movement is typically represented by velocity (rate of change of position) and acceleration (rate of change of velocity).[2]

- These values are updated over time based on forces acting on the object.
- Using vectors for velocity and acceleration allows for movement in any direction.[3]
- Euler Integration:
  - Euler integration is a simple numerical integration method used to update object positions and velocities over time.[4]
  - It involves calculating the new position and velocity based on the current values and the time step (delta time).
  - Euler integration can introduce inaccuracies, especially with large time steps, but it's often sufficient for basic game physics.[5]

- Implementing Movement:
  - Store object position, velocity, and acceleration as vectors.
  - In the update loop, update velocity based on acceleration: velocity += acceleration * deltaTime;
  - Update position based on velocity: position += velocity * deltaTime;[6]
  - Consider adding damping or friction to simulate realistic movement.
- Kinematics:
  - Kinematics describes the motion of objects without considering the forces that cause the motion.[7]
  - In game development, kinematics is often used to implement simple movement patterns or animations.

- Forces:
  - Forces are used to change the velocity of objects.[8]
  - Forces can be applied by the player, the environment, or other game objects.
  - Newton's second law of motion (F = ma) is used to calculate the acceleration of an object based on the forces acting on it.[9]
- Gravity:
  - Constant Acceleration:
    - Gravity is typically simulated as a constant downward acceleration.
    - This acceleration is added to the object's existing acceleration in the update loop.
  - Implementing Gravity:
    - Define a gravity vector (e.g., gravity = (0, -9.81)).

- In the update loop, add the gravity vector to the object's acceleration: acceleration += gravity;
- Consider adjusting the gravity value based on the game's scale and desired effect.
  - Projectile Motion:
    - Projectile motion involves simulating the trajectory of an object under the influence of gravity.[10]
    - This is often used for simulating projectiles like arrows, bullets, and grenades.
    - Projectile motion can be calculated using kinematic equations or numerical integration.[11]
  - Variable Gravity:
    - Some games require variable gravity, such as in

space environments or when simulating planetary gravity.
  - Variable gravity can be implemented by calculating the gravity vector based on the object's position and the gravitational forces of other objects.
- Integrating Forces:
  - When multiple forces are applied to an object, they are added together to calculate the net force.[12]
  - The net force is then used to calculate the object's acceleration.[13]
  - This is very important for complex physics simulations.
- Considerations:
  - Delta Time: Always use delta time to ensure consistent

physics simulations regardless of the frame rate.

- Units: Use consistent units for position, velocity, acceleration, and forces.
- Numerical Stability: Choose appropriate numerical integration methods and time step sizes to ensure numerical stability.
- Optimization: Optimize physics simulations to minimize CPU usage, especially for games with many moving objects.[14]

8.2 Collision Detection Algorithms (AABB, Sphere, Polygon)

Collision detection is essential for creating interactive and responsive game environments.

- Axis-Aligned Bounding Boxes (AABB):
  - Concept:

- An AABB is a rectangular box aligned with the coordinate axes that encloses an object.[15]
- AABBs are simple and efficient for collision detection.[16]
- Implementation:
  - Store the minimum and maximum coordinates of the AABB.
  - Check for overlap between two AABBs by comparing their minimum and maximum coordinates along each axis.
- Use Cases:
  - Simple collision detection for objects with rectangular shapes.
  - Preliminary collision detection for more complex shapes.
- Advantages:

- Very fast.
- Simple to implement.
  - Disadvantages:
    - Not very accurate for rotated objects.
- Spheres:
  - Concept:
    - A sphere is a simple geometric shape that can be used to approximate the shape of many objects.
    - Sphere collision detection is efficient and relatively accurate.
  - Implementation:
    - Store the center and radius of the sphere.
    - Check for collisions between two spheres by comparing the distance between their centers to the sum of their radii.
  - Use Cases:

- Collision detection for objects with spherical shapes.
- Approximating the shape of complex objects.
  - Advantages:
    - Fast.
    - Rotation invariant.
  - Disadvantages:
    - Not very accurate for elongated or complex shapes.
- Polygon Collision Detection:
  - Concept:
    - Polygon collision detection involves checking for overlap between two polygons.[17]
    - This is more complex than AABB or sphere collision detection but provides greater accuracy.
  - Implementation:

- Use techniques like the separating axis theorem (SAT) to check for polygon overlap.[18]
- SAT involves projecting the polygons onto a set of axes and checking for overlap along each axis.
  - Use Cases:
    - Collision detection for objects with arbitrary shapes.
    - Accurate collision detection for complex environments.
  - Advantages:
    - Very accurate.
  - Disadvantages:
    - Can be computationally expensive.
    - Complex to implement.
- Collision Response:
  - After a collision is detected, a collision response is calculated

to determine how the objects should react.[19]

- ○ Collision response can involve changing the velocities of the objects, applying forces, or triggering events.
- ○ This is very important for creating realistic interactions.
- Considerations:
  - ○ Performance: Choose appropriate collision detection algorithms based on the complexity of the game and the number of objects.
  - ○ Accuracy: Balance performance and accuracy based on the game's requirements.
  - ○ Optimization: Optimize collision detection algorithms to minimize CPU usage.[20]
  - ○ Broad Phase and Narrow Phase:
    - ■ Broad phase collision detection, is used to quickly eliminate pairs of

objects that are not colliding.[21]

- Narrow phase collision detection, is used to accurately detect collisions between pairs of objects that are potentially colliding.[22]

By mastering these fundamental concepts and techniques, game developers can create realistic and engaging game environments that respond to player actions and simulate the laws of physics.

8.3 Physics Engines: Integrating Libraries (Box2D, PhysX, Bullet)

Physics engines are libraries that provide pre-built physics simulation and collision detection functionalities, significantly simplifying game development.

- Box2D:
  - Overview:
    - Box2D is a 2D physics engine designed for

simulating rigid body dynamics in 2D games.[1]
- It's open-source and widely used for its stability, performance, and ease of use.[2]
  - Features:
    - Rigid body simulation.[3]
    - Collision detection and response.
    - Joints (e.g., revolute, prismatic, distance).[4]
    - Friction and restitution.
    - Ray casting and shape queries.
  - Integration:
    - Box2D is typically integrated as a library into the game's codebase.
    - Game objects are represented as Box2D bodies, and their properties are synchronized between the

game and the physics engine.[5]
- Box2D is very well documented.
- Use Cases:
  - 2D platformers, puzzle games, and other 2D games requiring realistic physics.
- PhysX:
  - Overview:
    - PhysX is a powerful 3D physics engine developed by NVIDIA.[6]
    - It's widely used in AAA games for its advanced features and performance.[7]
  - Features:
    - Rigid body and soft body simulation.
    - Collision detection and response.
    - Particle systems and fluid dynamics.

- Destructible environments.
- Vehicle physics.
  - Integration:
    - PhysX is integrated as a library or SDK into the game.[8]
    - It can be accelerated by NVIDIA GPUs for improved performance.[9]
    - PhysX has a large feature set.
  - Use Cases:
    - AAA games, simulations, and other 3D applications requiring advanced physics.[10]
- Bullet Physics Library:
  - Overview:
    - Bullet is a cross-platform, open-source 3D physics engine.[11]

- It's known for its versatility and performance.
  - Features:
    - Rigid body and soft body simulation.
    - Collision detection and response.
    - Constraints and joints.
    - Vehicle physics.
    - Discrete and continuous collision detection.
  - Integration:
    - Bullet is integrated as a library into the game.
    - It provides a flexible API for customizing physics simulations.
    - Bullet is very portable.[12]
  - Use Cases:
    - 3D games, simulations, and robotics applications.
- Benefits of Using Physics Engines:

- Reduced Development Time: Physics engines provide pre-built functionality, saving developers time and effort.[13]
- Realistic Physics: Physics engines simulate realistic physics phenomena, enhancing game immersion.[14]
- Performance Optimization: Physics engines are optimized for performance, ensuring smooth gameplay.[15]
- Feature-Rich: Physics engines offer a wide range of features, enabling complex physics simulations.[16]

8.4 Implementing Game Physics for Realistic Interactions

Creating realistic interactions requires careful consideration of physics principles and game design.

- Collision Response:
  - Elastic Collisions:

- Elastic collisions conserve kinetic energy, resulting in objects bouncing off each other with minimal energy loss.[17]
  - Inelastic Collisions:
    - Inelastic collisions involve energy loss, resulting in objects sticking together or deforming upon impact.[18]
  - Friction:
    - Friction simulates the resistance between surfaces in contact.[19]
    - Static friction prevents objects from sliding until a certain force is applied.[20]
    - Kinetic friction slows down moving objects.[21]
  - Restitution:
    - Restitution determines the bounciness of objects during collisions.

- A restitution value of 1.0 results in perfectly elastic collisions.[22]
- A restitution value of 0.0 results in perfectly inelastic collisions.[23]
  - Implementing realistic collision responses, is very important for believable game worlds.
- Constraints and Joints:
  - Joints:
    - Joints connect rigid bodies, allowing for constrained motion.[24]
    - Examples include revolute joints, prismatic joints, and distance joints.
  - Constraints:
    - Constraints enforce specific relationships between objects, such as limiting their relative motion.[25]

- Constraints are used to simulate realistic interactions, such as hinges, ropes, and chains.[26]
- Destructible Environments:
  - Fracturing and Fragmentation:
    - Destructible environments involve breaking objects into smaller pieces upon impact.
    - Techniques like Voronoi fracturing and particle systems are used to simulate realistic destruction.[27]
  - Damage Modeling:
    - Damage modeling involves simulating the effects of damage on objects, such as cracks, dents, and deformations.

- This can be done using vertex shaders, or by pre-fracturing objects.
- Vehicle Physics:
  - Tire Friction and Suspension:
    - Vehicle physics involves simulating the behavior of vehicles, including tire friction, suspension, and aerodynamics.
    - This is essential for racing games and other vehicle-based simulations.
  - Aerodynamics:
    - Simulating wind resistance, and the effects of air on vehicles.
- Ragdoll Physics:
  - Skeletal Animation and Physics:
    - Ragdoll physics involves simulating the physics of character bodies, allowing for realistic death

animations and interactions.[28]

- This is often done by combining skeletal animation with rigid body physics.

- Fluid Dynamics:
  - Particle-Based Fluids:
    - Particle-based fluid simulations involve simulating fluids as a collection of particles.[29]
    - This is often used for simulating water, smoke, and other fluid effects.[30]
  - Grid-Based Fluids:
    - Grid based fluid simulations, calculate the movement of fluids, based on a grid.[31]

- Considerations:
  - Performance: Optimize physics simulations to minimize CPU

usage, especially for games with many interacting objects.

- ○ Stability: Choose appropriate physics parameters and simulation settings to ensure stability and prevent unrealistic behavior.
- ○ Game Design: Balance realism and gameplay by adjusting physics parameters to create enjoyable and engaging experiences.
- ○ Debugging Physics: Physics simulations can be difficult to debug. Using visual debugging tools is essential.

By mastering these advanced physics concepts and techniques, game developers can create realistic and immersive game environments that respond to player actions and simulate the laws of physics.

CHAPTER 9

Audio Programming and Sound Effects

Audio programming in game development is crucial for creating immersive experiences. Effective use of sound effects and music playback, coupled with 3D audio and spatialization, enhances player engagement. Audio libraries like OpenAL, FMOD, and Wwise offer tools for managing audio resources. Proper mixing and effects are essential for achieving high-quality soundscapes, contributing significantly to a game's overall polish and emotional impact.

9.1 Integrating Audio Libraries (OpenAL, FMOD, Wwise)

Audio libraries provide powerful tools for managing and playing audio in game environments.[1]

- OpenAL (Open Audio Library):

- Overview:
  - OpenAL is a cross-platform, open-source audio API that provides 3D spatial audio capabilities.[2]
  - It's designed to be similar to OpenGL, providing a standardized interface for audio rendering.[3]
- Features:
  - 3D spatial audio.
  - Multi-channel audio playback.
  - Doppler effect simulation.
  - Environmental audio effects.
- Integration:
  - OpenAL is typically integrated as a library into the game's codebase.
  - It provides a low-level API for managing audio buffers and sources.[4]

- - OpenAL is well supported on many platforms.[5]
  - Use Cases:
    - Games requiring 3D spatial audio and environmental effects.
    - Cross-platform games.
  - Advantages:
    - Cross-platform.
    - Open source.
    - 3D audio support.
  - Disadvantages:
    - Lower level than FMOD or Wwise.
    - Requires more code to get similar results.
- FMOD (Fast Object-Oriented Media System):
  - Overview:
    - FMOD is a powerful and versatile audio engine that provides a high-level API for audio playback and processing.

- It's widely used in the game industry for its advanced features and ease of use.
  - Features:
    - 3D spatial audio.
    - Advanced mixing and effects.
    - Dynamic sound parameters.
    - Virtual voice management.
    - Audio middleware capabilities.
  - Integration:
    - FMOD is integrated as a library or SDK into the game.
    - It provides a flexible and intuitive API for managing audio resources and events.
    - FMOD has excellent documentation.[6]
  - Use Cases:

- AAA games, simulations, and other applications requiring advanced audio features.
    - Advantages:
        - High level API.
        - Feature rich.
        - Excellent tooling.
    - Disadvantages:
        - Commercial license.
- Wwise (Audiokinetic Wwise):
    - Overview:
        - Wwise is a comprehensive audio middleware solution that provides a powerful and flexible audio pipeline.[7]
        - It's widely used in the game industry for its advanced features and workflow.
    - Features:
        - 3D spatial audio.

- Interactive music and sound design.
- Advanced mixing and effects.
- Real-time parameter control.
- Audio authoring tools.
- Integration:
  - Wwise is integrated as a library and authoring tool into the game's development pipeline.[8]
  - It provides a visual interface for managing audio assets and events.
  - Wwise is very powerful.
- Use Cases:
  - AAA games, simulations, and other applications requiring advanced audio authoring and interactive sound design.[9]
- Advantages:
  - Very powerful.

- ■ Excellent authoring tools.
- ■ Designed for game audio.
  - ○ Disadvantages:
    - ■ Commercial license.
    - ■ Steep learning curve.
- Choosing an Audio Library:
  - ○ Project Requirements: Consider the specific audio requirements of the game, such as 3D spatial audio, interactive music, or advanced effects.
  - ○ Platform Support: Ensure that the chosen audio library supports the target platforms.
  - ○ Budget: Evaluate the licensing costs of commercial audio libraries.
  - ○ Ease of Use: Consider the learning curve and ease of integration of the audio library.
  - ○ Performance: Evaluate the performance of the audio library, especially for games with high audio demands.

9.2 Sound Effects and Music Playback: Managing Audio Resources

Efficiently managing audio resources is essential for creating immersive and performant audio experiences.

- Sound Effects:
  - File Formats:
    - Use appropriate audio file formats (e.g., WAV, Ogg Vorbis, MP3) to optimize file size and quality.
    - Consider using compressed audio formats for background music and long sound effects.
  - Sound Buffers:
    - Load sound effects into audio buffers for efficient playback.
    - Use streaming buffers for large audio files to avoid

loading the entire file into
memory.

- Sound Sources:
  - Create sound sources to
    represent the position and
    properties of sound effects.
  - Adjust sound source
    parameters (e.g., volume,
    pitch, panning) to create
    dynamic audio effects.
- Attenuation and Spatialization:
  - Use attenuation to
    simulate the distance and
    direction of sound sources.
  - Use spatialization to create
    3D audio effects.
- Looping and Triggering:
  - Implement looping for
    ambient sounds and
    background music.
  - Trigger sound effects
    based on game events and
    player actions.
- Sound Effects Pools:

- Use sound effect pools, to reduce the amount of audio creation, and destruction.
- Music Playback:
    - Streaming Music:
        - Stream background music from disk to avoid loading the entire file into memory.
        - This is important for large music files.
    - Crossfading and Transitioning:
        - Implement crossfading and transitioning between music tracks to create smooth transitions.
        - This is important for dynamic music systems.
    - Interactive Music:
        - Create interactive music systems that adapt to game events and player actions.

- This can involve changing music tracks, adjusting music parameters, or triggering sound effects.
  - Music Volume Control:
    - Provide options for adjusting music volume separately from sound effect volume.
    - This allows players to customize their audio preferences.
- Audio Resource Management:
  - Audio Asset Organization:
    - Organize audio assets in a logical and hierarchical manner.
    - Use descriptive file names and metadata to facilitate asset management.
  - Audio Caching:
    - Implement audio caching to avoid reloading audio

assets that are already in memory.

- Use a least recently used (LRU) cache to manage the audio cache.

○ Memory Management:
- Manage audio memory efficiently to avoid memory leaks and performance issues.
- Use smart pointers or other resource management techniques.

○ Audio Profiling:
- Profile audio performance to identify bottlenecks and optimize audio playback.
- This can involve measuring CPU usage, memory usage, and audio latency.

○ Audio Threading:

- Offload audio processing to a separate thread to improve performance.
- This is particularly important for games with complex audio systems.

By mastering audio library integration and audio resource management, game developers can create immersive and engaging audio experiences that enhance the player's emotional connection to the game world.

9.3 3D Audio and Spatialization: Creating Immersive Soundscapes

3D audio and spatialization techniques are essential for placing sounds in a 3D environment, enhancing immersion and providing positional cues to the player.[1]

- 3D Audio Concepts:
  - Listener and Source Positions:
    - 3D audio systems simulate the positions of the

listener (player) and sound sources in a 3D space.[2]

- This allows for accurate panning and attenuation of sounds based on their relative positions.

- Doppler Effect:
  - The Doppler effect simulates the change in pitch of a sound source as it moves relative to the listener.[3]
  - This effect is crucial for creating realistic movement sounds.[4]

- Attenuation:
  - Attenuation simulates the decrease in sound volume as the distance between the listener and sound source increases.
  - This effect is essential for creating a sense of depth and distance.

- Directional Audio:
  - Directional audio involves focusing sound in a specific direction, simulating the directionality of real-world sound sources.[5]
  - This is often used for simulating sound cones and spotlights.
- Spatialization Techniques:
  - Panning:
    - Panning involves distributing sound between the left and right speakers based on the sound source's position.
    - This creates a sense of horizontal direction.
  - Elevation:
    - Elevation involves adjusting the balance between front and rear speakers to simulate the

vertical position of a sound source.

- This creates a sense of vertical direction.

o Distance Attenuation:

- Distance attenuation involves reducing the volume of a sound source based on its distance from the listener.[6]

- This creates a sense of depth and distance.

o Environmental Reverb:

- Environmental reverb simulates the reverberation of sound in different environments, such as rooms, hallways, and outdoor spaces.[7]

- This enhances the realism and immersion of the soundscape.

o Occlusion and Obstruction:

- Occlusion involves blocking sound by objects in the environment, simulating the way that sound is muffled or blocked by walls and other obstacles.
- Obstruction simulates the way that sound is attenuated or filtered by objects in the environment.[8]
  - HRTF (Head-Related Transfer Function):
    - HRTF involves using filters that simulate the way that sound is modified by the listener's head and ears.[9]
    - This creates a more realistic and immersive 3D audio experience.
- Implementing 3D Audio:
  - Audio Libraries:

- Use audio libraries like OpenAL, FMOD, or Wwise to implement 3D audio and spatialization.[10]
- These libraries provide functions for setting listener and source positions, adjusting attenuation, and applying environmental effects.
  - Audio Engines:
    - Game engines often provide built-in 3D audio systems.
    - These systems typically abstract away the complexities of audio library integration.
  - Audio Middleware:
    - Audio middleware like Wwise provides advanced tools for creating and managing 3D audio soundscapes.[11]

- These tools allow for fine-grained control over sound source properties and environmental effects.
- Benefits of 3D Audio:
  - Enhanced Immersion: 3D audio creates a more realistic and immersive soundscape, enhancing the player's sense of presence.[12]
  - Positional Cues: 3D audio provides positional cues to the player, allowing them to locate sound sources and navigate the environment.[13]
  - Improved Gameplay: 3D audio can enhance gameplay by providing tactical information and creating a more dynamic and engaging experience.[14]

9.4 Mixing and Effects: Enhancing Audio Quality

Mixing and effects are essential for creating high-quality and polished audio experiences in games.[15]

- Audio Mixing:
  - Balancing Sound Levels:
    - Audio mixing involves adjusting the volume levels of different sound sources to create a balanced and cohesive soundscape.[16]
    - This ensures that important sounds are audible and that the overall soundscape is pleasing to the ear.
  - Panning and Spatialization:
    - Panning and spatialization are used to place sounds in the stereo or 3D soundscape.[17]

- - This creates a sense of space and direction.
  - Equalization (EQ):
    - EQ involves adjusting the frequency content of sound sources to shape their tonal balance.[18]
    - This can be used to enhance specific frequencies, reduce unwanted frequencies, or create unique sound effects.
  - Compression:
    - Compression involves reducing the dynamic range of sound sources to create a more consistent and polished sound.[19]
    - This can be used to increase the perceived loudness of sounds and prevent clipping.
  - Mastering:

- - Mastering involves applying final adjustments to the overall soundscape to ensure that it is consistent and polished.
  - This can involve adjusting the overall volume, applying compression and EQ, and adding final effects.[20]
- Audio Effects:
  - Reverb:
    - Reverb simulates the reverberation of sound in different environments.[21]
    - This can be used to create a sense of space and depth.
  - Delay:
    - Delay involves creating echoes of a sound source.
    - This can be used to create rhythmic effects and enhance the sense of space.

- Chorus:
    - Chorus involves creating multiple copies of a sound source and slightly detuning them.
    - This creates a rich and spacious sound.
- Flanger and Phaser:
    - Flanger and phaser effects create swirling and whooshing sounds.[22]
    - These effects are often used for creating sci-fi and psychedelic sounds.
- Distortion:
    - Distortion involves adding harmonic distortion to a sound source.
    - This can be used to create aggressive and gritty sounds.
- Filters:
    - Filters are used to remove or enhance specific

frequencies in a sound source.[23]

- This can be used to create a variety of effects, such as low-pass filters for simulating muffled sounds and high-pass filters for creating bright and airy sounds.

- Implementing Mixing and Effects:
  - Audio Libraries:
    - Use audio libraries like FMOD or Wwise to implement mixing and effects.[24]
    - These libraries provide functions for adjusting sound source parameters and applying audio effects.
  - Audio Engines:
    - Game engines often provide built-in audio mixing and effects systems.[25]

- These systems typically provide a visual interface for adjusting sound parameters and applying effects.
  - Audio Middleware:
    - Audio middleware like Wwise provides advanced tools for creating and managing audio mixing and effects.[26]
    - These tools allow for fine-grained control over sound parameters and effects.
- Benefits of Mixing and Effects:
  - Enhanced Audio Quality: Mixing and effects enhance the overall quality of the audio experience.[27]
  - Improved Immersion: Mixing and effects create a more realistic and immersive soundscape.[28]

- Creative Sound Design: Mixing and effects allow for creative sound design and experimentation.[29]
- Professional Sounding Games: Polished audio is very important for a professional feeling game.

By mastering 3D audio, spatialization, mixing, and effects, game developers can create immersive and high-quality audio experiences that enhance the player's emotional connection to the game world.

CHAPTER 10

Networking and Multiplayer Game Development

Networking and multiplayer game development presents unique challenges and opportunities. Understanding network protocols (TCP/IP, UDP) and client-server architecture is foundational.[1] Robust networking requires careful handling of latency and packet loss through techniques like prediction and interpolation. State synchronization ensures consistent game experiences across players.[2] Ultimately, successful multiplayer games demand a balance between performance, reliability, and security, creating immersive and engaging online environments.

10.1 Network Protocols: TCP/IP, UDP, and Socket Programming

Understanding network protocols and socket programming is essential for creating robust and efficient multiplayer games.[1]

- TCP/IP (Transmission Control Protocol/Internet Protocol):
  - Overview:
    - TCP/IP is a suite of communication protocols used to connect network devices on the internet.[2]
    - It provides reliable, ordered, and error-checked delivery of data.[3]
  - TCP (Transmission Control Protocol):
    - TCP is a connection-oriented protocol that establishes a reliable connection between two endpoints.[4]

- It ensures that data is delivered in the correct order and without errors.[5]
- TCP is suitable for applications that require reliable data transfer, such as chat, file transfers, and turn-based games.[6]
- TCP is very reliable, but slower than UDP.[7]
- IP (Internet Protocol):
  - IP is a connectionless protocol that handles the addressing and routing of data packets.[8]
  - It's responsible for delivering data packets from one network to another.[9]
- Use Cases in Games:
  - Turn-based strategy games.

- - - MMOs (Massively Multiplayer Online games) for critical data.
    - Chat systems.
    - File transfers.
  - Advantages:
    - Reliable data delivery.
    - Ordered data delivery.
    - Error checking and retransmission.
  - Disadvantages:
    - Higher overhead and latency.
    - Slower data transfer.
- UDP (User Datagram Protocol):
  - Overview:
    - UDP is a connectionless protocol that provides fast and efficient data transfer.[10]
    - It does not guarantee data delivery or order.[11]
    - UDP is suitable for applications that require

low latency and high throughput, such as real-time games and video streaming.[12]

- ○ Use Cases in Games:
  - Real-time action games (FPS, racing).
  - Voice chat.
  - Streaming game data.
- ○ Advantages:
  - Low overhead and latency.
  - Fast data transfer.
- ○ Disadvantages:
  - Unreliable data delivery.
  - Unordered data delivery.
  - No error checking or retransmission.
- Socket Programming:
  - ○ Overview:
    - Socket programming is the process of creating network applications using sockets, which are endpoints for

communication between two devices.[13]

- Sockets provide an interface for sending and receiving data over a network.[14]
  - Socket Types:
    - TCP Sockets (SOCK_STREAM): Used for reliable, connection-oriented communication.
    - UDP Sockets (SOCK_DGRAM): Used for unreliable, connectionless communication.[15]
  - Socket Operations:
    - Creating Sockets: Allocating resources for network communication.
    - Binding Sockets: Associating a socket with a local address and port.[16]

- Listening for Connections (TCP): Accepting incoming connection requests.
- Connecting to Servers (TCP): Establishing a connection with a remote server.
- Sending and Receiving Data: Transmitting and receiving data over the network.
- Closing Sockets: Releasing network resources.
  - Cross-Platform Socket Programming:
    - Platform specific differences exist, so abstraction layers are often used.
    - Libraries like SDL_net or Boost.Asio allow for cross platform socket programming.[17]
  - Considerations:

- Network security is very important.
- Handling network errors is essential.
- Properly closing sockets is important for resource management.

10.2 Client-Server Architecture: Designing Networked Games

Client-server architecture is a common design pattern for multiplayer games, where a central server manages the game state and clients connect to the server to participate in the game.[18]

- Client-Server Model:
  - Server:
    - The server is a central authority that manages the game state, handles player input, and broadcasts game updates to clients.[19]

- The server is responsible for enforcing game rules and preventing cheating.[20]
- The server must be very reliable.
  - Client:
    - The client is a player's device that connects to the server and displays the game world.[21]
    - The client sends player input to the server and receives game updates from the server.[22]
    - The client renders the game world, based on the server information.[23]
- Server Types:
  - Authoritative Server:
    - The server has complete control over the game state, and clients trust the server's data.[24]

- - This model is used for games where cheating is a major concern.
  - Non-Authoritative Server:
    - The server acts as a relay, and clients have some control over the game state.
    - This model is used for games where latency is a major concern.
  - Dedicated Servers:
    - Servers that are only used to host the game.
  - Listen Servers:
    - Servers that are hosted by one of the players.
- Client-Server Communication:
  - Data Serialization:
    - Data serialization involves converting game data into a format that can be transmitted over the network.[25]

- Common serialization formats include JSON, XML, and binary formats.[26]
- Data Deserialization:
  - Converting the network data, back into a game readable format.
- Network Messages:
  - Network messages are used to communicate between the client and the server.
  - Messages can contain player input, game updates, and other data.
- Message Queues:
  - Message queues, are used to handle network messages asynchronously.[27]
- Latency Compensation:
  - Latency compensation techniques, are used to

hide the effects of network latency.[28]

- Benefits of Client-Server Architecture:
  - Centralized Game State: The server manages the game state, ensuring consistency and preventing cheating.[29]
  - Scalability: The server can handle a large number of clients.
  - Security: The server can enforce game rules and prevent cheating.[30]
  - Easier Updates: Game updates can be deployed to the server without requiring client updates.
- Challenges of Client-Server Architecture:
  - Latency: Network latency can affect gameplay.[31]
  - Server Load: The server must handle a large number of clients.
  - Network Security: The server must be protected from attacks.

○ Development Complexity: Client-server architecture adds complexity to game development.

By understanding network protocols and client-server architecture, game developers can create engaging and scalable multiplayer games that provide immersive online experiences.

10.3 Handling Latency and Packet Loss: Implementing Robust Networking

Latency and packet loss are inherent challenges in network programming, and robust handling of these issues is crucial for creating smooth and enjoyable multiplayer experiences.

- **Latency:**
  - ○ **Definition:** Latency is the delay between sending a network message and receiving a response.

- Impact: Latency can cause noticeable delays in gameplay, leading to jerky movement, delayed actions, and desynchronization.[1]
- Mitigation Techniques:
  - **Latency Compensation:** Techniques like client-side prediction and server-side reconciliation can help hide the effects of latency.[2]
  - **Dead Reckoning:** Clients predict the future positions of objects based on their current velocity and acceleration.[3]
  - **Prioritization of Critical Data:** Send critical game data (e.g., player movement, actions) with higher priority.[4]
  - **Region-Based Servers:** Use servers that are

geographically close to players to minimize latency.

- **Reducing Packet Size:** Smaller packets are sent faster.[5]
- **Optimizing Network Code:** Properly written network code is essential.

○ **Ping and Network Diagnostics:**

- Implement ping functionality to measure latency and provide feedback to players.
- Provide network diagnostics tools to help players troubleshoot network issues.

- **Packet Loss:**
  ○ **Definition:** Packet loss occurs when network messages are lost during transmission.[6]

- Impact: Packet loss can cause missing game updates, desynchronization, and unpredictable behavior.[7]
- **Mitigation Techniques:**
  - **Reliable Protocols (TCP):** Use TCP for critical data that must be delivered reliably.
  - **Redundancy:** Send redundant data to increase the likelihood of successful delivery.
  - **Error Correction:** Use error correction codes to recover lost or corrupted data.
  - **Packet Acknowledgments:** Implement packet acknowledgments to detect and retransmit lost packets.

- **Interpolation:** Smooth out missing data by interpolating between received packets.
- **Rate Limiting:** Control the rate of packets being sent.
- **Packet Buffering:** Buffering packets, allows for the smoothing of network traffic.[8]
  - **UDP Reliability Layers:**
    - Implement reliability layers on top of UDP to provide features like packet acknowledgments and retransmission.
    - Libraries like ENet provide reliable UDP functionality.[9]
- **Jitter:**
  - **Definition:** Jitter is the variation in latency over time.[10]

- o **Impact:** Jitter can cause inconsistent gameplay and jerky movement.[11]
- o **Mitigation Techniques:**
  - ▪ **Jitter Buffers:** Use jitter buffers to smooth out variations in latency.[12]
  - ▪ **Interpolation:** Interpolate between received packets to smooth out jitter.
- **Network Security:**
  - o **Encryption:** Use encryption to protect network traffic from eavesdropping and tampering.[13]
  - o **Authentication:** Implement authentication mechanisms to verify the identity of players and servers.
  - o **Anti-Cheat Measures:** Implement anti-cheat measures to prevent players from gaining unfair advantages.[14]
- **Network Bandwidth:**

- ○ **Optimizing Data Transmission:** Minimize the amount of data transmitted over the network.[15]
- ○ **Data Compression:** Use data compression techniques to reduce packet size.
- ○ **Data Culling:** Only send data that is relevant to the client.

10.4 State Synchronization and Prediction: Ensuring Smooth Multiplayer Experiences

State synchronization and prediction are crucial for creating smooth and responsive multiplayer experiences, especially in games with high latency.

- **State Synchronization:**
  - ○ **Definition:** State synchronization involves keeping the game states of all

clients and the server consistent.[16]

- ○ **Techniques:**
  - **Snapshot Interpolation:** Clients interpolate between received snapshots of the game state to smooth out movement and actions.
  - **Entity Interpolation:** Interpolate the position, rotation, and other properties of individual game entities.
  - **State Compression:** Compress game state data to reduce network bandwidth usage.
  - **Delta Compression:** only send the changes to the game state.
  - **Reliable State Transfer:** Use reliable network protocols, or

reliable layers on top of UDP, to ensure that all state updates are received.

- **Server Reconciliation:**
  - The server corrects client-side predictions based on authoritative server data.
  - This helps prevent cheating and ensures that the game state remains consistent.

- **Client-Side Prediction:**
  - **Definition:** Client-side prediction involves predicting the future state of the game world based on client input.[17]
  - **Techniques:**
    - **Dead Reckoning:** Clients predict the future positions of objects based on their current velocity and acceleration.[18]

- **Input Prediction:** Clients predict the effects of their own actions before receiving confirmation from the server.[19]
- **Extrapolation:** Clients predict the future state of objects by extrapolating their current movement and behavior.[20]

○ **Benefits:**
- Reduces the perceived latency of player actions.
- Creates a more responsive and fluid gameplay experience.

○ **Challenges:**
- Can lead to visual discrepancies when client predictions are corrected by the server.
- Requires careful implementation to avoid excessive correction.

- **Extrapolation vs. Interpolation:**
  - **Extrapolation:** Predicting future state, used for client side prediction.
  - **Interpolation:** Smoothing between known states, used for state synchronization.[21]
- **Time Synchronization:**
  - Maintaining a consistent time across all clients and the server is essential for accurate state synchronization.
  - NTP (Network Time Protocol) or custom time synchronization mechanisms can be used.[22]
- **Considerations:**
  - **Game Genre:** The choice of state synchronization and prediction techniques depends on the game genre and gameplay requirements.
  - **Network Latency:** Higher latency requires more aggressive

prediction and compensation techniques.

- ○ **Computational Cost:** State synchronization and prediction can be computationally expensive.
- ○ **Network Bandwidth:** Efficient state synchronization minimizes network bandwidth usage.[23]

By mastering these advanced networking concepts and techniques, game developers can create smooth, responsive, and engaging multiplayer experiences that overcome the challenges of latency and packet loss.

Part III:

Advanced Game Development Techniques

CHAPTER 11

Game AI and Pathfinding

Game AI and pathfinding are critical components in creating engaging and immersive game experiences. AI encompasses simulating intelligent behaviors through techniques like Finite State Machines, Behavior Trees, and advanced decision-making processes.

Pathfinding, utilizing algorithms such as A* and Dijkstra's, enables AI agents to navigate complex environments efficiently. Scripting languages like Lua and Python further enhance AI capabilities by allowing for dynamic behavior modification and extension of game logic. Effective AI design requires careful consideration of performance, real-time responsiveness, and alignment with overall game design principles.

11.1 Implementing Basic AI Behaviors (Finite State Machines, Behavior Trees)

Implementing basic AI behaviors is crucial for creating engaging and dynamic game characters.[1]

- Finite State Machines (FSMs):
  - Concept:
    - An FSM is a computational model that represents an AI agent's behavior as a set of states and transitions between those states.[2]
    - Each state represents a specific behavior, and transitions occur based on[3] predefined conditions.[4]
  - Implementation:
    - Define the states of the AI agent (e.g., idle, patrol, attack, flee).
    - Define the transitions between the states (e.g.,

when the enemy is sighted, transition from patrol to attack).
  - Implement the logic for each state (e.g., move towards the player in the attack state).
  - Use a state variable to track the current state of the AI agent.
- Advantages:
  - Simple to implement and understand.
  - Efficient for simple AI behaviors.
  - Very useful for basic AI.
- Disadvantages:
  - Can become complex for more sophisticated AI behaviors.
  - Not very flexible or scalable.
- Use Cases:

- Simple enemy AI (e.g., patrolling guards).[5]
- UI state management.
- Simple game logic.
- Behavior Trees (BTs):
  - Concept:
    - A BT is a hierarchical structure that represents an AI agent's behavior as a tree of nodes.[6]
    - Each node represents a task or condition, and the tree is traversed to determine the AI agent's actions.[7]
  - Node Types:
    - Sequences: Execute child nodes in order until one fails.[8]
    - Selectors: Execute child nodes in order until one succeeds.[9]

- Tasks: Perform specific actions (e.g., move, attack).[10]
- Conditions: Check conditions (e.g., is the player in range?).
- Decorators: Modify the behavior of child nodes (e.g., repeat, invert).
- Implementation:
  - Design the behavior tree structure using a visual editor or code.
  - Implement the logic for each node in the tree.
  - Traverse the tree to determine the AI agent's actions.
- Advantages:
  - More flexible and scalable than FSMs.[11]
  - Easier to create complex AI behaviors.
  - Easy to visualize.

- Disadvantages:
  - More complex to implement than FSMs.
  - Can be computationally expensive for very large trees.
- Use Cases:
  - Complex enemy AI (e.g., intelligent opponents).
  - Character behavior in simulations.
  - Any complex AI.
- Hybrid Approaches:
  - Combine FSMs and BTs to create more sophisticated AI behaviors.
  - Use FSMs for simple state management and BTs for complex decision-making.[12]
  - This allows for the benefits of both systems.
- Considerations:
  - Performance: Choose appropriate AI techniques based

on the complexity of the game and the number of AI agents.

- ○ Maintainability: Design AI systems that are easy to understand and modify.
- ○ Game Design: Ensure that AI behaviors align with the game's design and enhance the player experience.
- ○ Debugging AI: AI can be difficult to debug. Use visual debugging tools and logging to identify and resolve issues.

11.2 Pathfinding Algorithms (A, Dijkstra's Algorithm)*

Pathfinding algorithms are essential for enabling AI agents to navigate through complex environments.[13]

- Dijkstra's Algorithm:
  - ○ Concept:
    - ■ Dijkstra's algorithm is a graph search algorithm that finds the shortest path

between two nodes in a weighted graph.[14]

- It explores the graph by iteratively expanding the node with the lowest cost.

○ Implementation:

- Create a graph representation of the game environment (e.g., a grid or navigation mesh).

- Initialize the cost of the start node to 0 and the cost of all other nodes to infinity.

- Use a priority queue to store nodes based on their cost.

- Iteratively expand the node with the lowest cost and update the costs of its neighbors.

- Terminate when the goal node is reached.

○ Advantages:

- Guaranteed to find the shortest path.
- Works well for graphs with non-negative edge weights.
  - Disadvantages:
    - Can be computationally expensive for large graphs.
    - Explores nodes in all directions.
  - Use Cases:
    - Finding the shortest path in a static environment.
    - Navigation in turn-based strategy games.
- A Algorithm:*
  - Concept:
    - The A* algorithm is a graph search algorithm that finds the shortest path between two nodes in a weighted graph.[15]
    - It uses a heuristic function to estimate the cost of

reaching the goal node, guiding the search towards the goal.

- Implementation:
  - Similar to Dijkstra's algorithm, but uses a heuristic function to prioritize nodes.
  - The heuristic function estimates the cost of reaching the goal node from a given node.
- Advantages:
  - More efficient than Dijkstra's algorithm for many problems.
  - Finds the shortest path in most cases.
- Disadvantages:
  - The heuristic function must be admissible (never overestimates the cost).[16]

- Can be computationally expensive for very large graphs.
  - Use Cases:
    - Real-time pathfinding in dynamic environments.
    - Navigation in first-person shooters and real-time strategy games.
- Heuristic Functions:
  - Manhattan Distance: Used for grid-based environments.
  - Euclidean Distance: Used for continuous environments.
  - Diagonal Distance: Used for grid-based environments with diagonal movement.
- Navigation Meshes (Navmeshes):
  - Navmeshes are polygon meshes that represent the walkable areas of a game environment.[17]
  - Pathfinding algorithms can be used to find paths along navmeshes.[18]

- Navmeshes are very efficient for pathfinding in complex environments.[19]
- Path Smoothing:
    - Path smoothing techniques are used to create smoother and more natural-looking paths.[20]
    - Techniques like spline interpolation and string pulling can be used.
- Considerations:
    - Performance: Choose appropriate pathfinding algorithms based on the complexity of the game and the number of AI agents.
    - Dynamic Environments: Implement pathfinding algorithms that can adapt to dynamic changes in the environment.
    - Real-Time Pathfinding: Optimize pathfinding algorithms for real-time performance.

- Memory Usage: Be mindful of memory usage when implementing pathfinding algorithms.

By mastering these AI behavior and pathfinding techniques, game developers can create intelligent and engaging AI agents that bring virtual worlds to life.

11.3 AI Perception and Decision-Making: Creating Intelligent Agents

Creating truly intelligent AI agents requires more than just basic behaviors and pathfinding; it demands robust perception and decision-making capabilities.

- AI Perception:
  - Sensory Input:
    - AI agents need to perceive their environment through simulated senses, such as vision, hearing, and touch.

- These senses provide the agent with information about the world around them.
- Raycasting:
  - Raycasting is a technique for simulating vision by casting rays from the AI agent's eyes to detect objects in the environment.
  - This allows the agent to determine if objects are visible and within its field of view.
- Sensor Data:
  - Sensor data can include information about object positions, distances, velocities, and other properties.
  - This data is used by the AI agent to make decisions.
- Object Recognition:

- Object recognition involves identifying and classifying objects in the environment.
- This can be done using techniques like pattern matching or machine learning.
- Environmental Awareness:
  - AI agents need to build and maintain a representation of their environment, including the positions of objects and other relevant information.
  - This allows the agent to reason about the world around them.
- Memory:
  - AI agents need to have memory to store information about past events and observations.

- This allows the agent to learn from its experiences and adapt its behavior.
- AI Decision-Making:
  - Goal-Oriented Behavior:
    - AI agents should have goals and objectives that drive their behavior.
    - These goals can be explicit (e.g., find the player) or implicit (e.g., maintain a safe distance).
  - Rule-Based Systems:
    - Rule-based systems use a set of rules to determine the AI agent's actions based on its perception of the environment.
    - These rules can be simple or complex.
  - Planning Algorithms:
    - Planning algorithms, like A* or Monte Carlo Tree Search (MCTS), can be

used to generate plans of action for the AI agent.
- These algorithms allow the agent to reason about the consequences of its actions.
- Utility-Based Decision Making:
  - Utility-based decision-making involves assigning a utility value to each possible action based on its desirability.
  - The AI agent selects the action with the highest utility.
- Machine Learning:
  - Machine learning techniques, such as reinforcement learning and neural networks, can be used to train AI agents to make decisions based on their experiences.

- This allows the agent to learn and adapt over time.
  - Hierarchical Decision Making:
    - Break down complex decisions into smaller, more manageable sub-decisions.
    - This can be implemented using behavior trees or hierarchical state machines.
  - Action Selection:
    - The process of choosing an action to take based on the AI agent's perception and decision-making.
    - This can involve selecting an action from a set of predefined actions or generating a new action.
- AI Learning:
  - Reinforcement Learning:
    - AI agents learn through trial and error by receiving

rewards for desirable actions and penalties for undesirable actions.

- This allows the agent to learn optimal strategies over time.

○ Supervised Learning:
  - AI agents learn from labeled data, such as examples of correct and incorrect actions.
  - This allows the agent to learn patterns and relationships in the data.

○ Unsupervised Learning:
  - AI agents learn from unlabeled data by finding patterns and structures in the data.
  - This allows the agent to discover hidden relationships and make predictions.

○ Evolutionary Algorithms:

- Evolutionary algorithms simulate the process of natural selection to evolve AI agents that are well-suited to their environment.
- Considerations:
  - Computational Cost: Perception and decision-making can be computationally expensive. Optimize algorithms and data structures to minimize CPU usage.
  - Real-Time Performance: Ensure that AI agents can make decisions in real-time without causing noticeable delays.
  - Game Design: Align AI behavior with the game's design and enhance the player experience.
  - Debugging AI: Debugging AI can be challenging. Use visual debugging tools and logging to identify and resolve issues.

11.4 Scripting AI with Lua or Python: Extending Game Logic

Scripting languages like Lua and Python provide a powerful way to extend game logic and create dynamic AI behaviors.

- Lua:
    - Overview:
        - Lua is a lightweight and fast scripting language that is well-suited for embedding in games.
        - It's known for its simplicity and efficiency.
    - Benefits:
        - Easy to learn and use.
        - Fast execution speed.
        - Small memory footprint.
        - Excellent for embedding in C++.
    - Use Cases:
        - Scripting AI behaviors.
        - Creating dynamic game events.

- Implementing game logic.
- Modifying game parameters at runtime.
- Python:
  - Overview:
    - Python is a versatile and powerful scripting language that is widely used in various domains, including game development.
    - It's known for its readability and extensive libraries.
  - Benefits:
    - Easy to learn and use.
    - Extensive libraries for various tasks.
    - Large and active community.
    - Powerful and versatile.
  - Use Cases:
    - Scripting complex AI behaviors.

- - Creating game tools and editors.
  - Implementing data-driven game logic.
  - Rapid prototyping.
- Scripting AI:
  - Behavior Trees:
    - Scripting languages can be used to define and manipulate behavior trees.
    - This allows for creating complex and dynamic AI behaviors.
  - Rule-Based Systems:
    - Scripting languages can be used to define and execute rule-based AI systems.
    - This allows for creating flexible and adaptable AI agents.
  - State Machines:
    - Scripting languages can be used to implement and manage state machines.

- This allows for creating AI agents with distinct behaviors.
    - Dynamic AI Parameters:
        - Scripting languages can be used to modify AI parameters at runtime, such as speed, aggression, and perception range.
        - This allows for creating dynamic and adaptive AI agents.
- Integrating Scripting Languages:
    - Embedding Scripting Engines:
        - Embed scripting engines into the game engine to allow for executing script code.
        - Libraries like LuaBridge and PyBind11 simplify the process of embedding scripting languages.
    - Exposing Game API:

- Expose game API functions and data structures to the scripting language.
- This allows scripts to interact with the game engine and modify game state.
    - Scripting Events:
        - Use scripting languages to define and trigger game events.
        - This allows for creating dynamic and interactive gameplay.
- Benefits of Scripting:
    - Rapid Prototyping: Scripting languages allow for rapid prototyping and iteration of AI behaviors.
    - Modularity: Scripting allows for creating modular and reusable AI components.

- o Flexibility: Scripting allows for easily modifying and extending AI behaviors without recompiling the game engine.
- o Dynamic Content: Scripting allows for creating dynamic and adaptive AI that can respond to changing game conditions.
- Considerations:
  - o Performance: Script execution can be slower than compiled code. Optimize scripts for performance.
  - o Security: Be mindful of security risks when allowing user-generated scripts.
  - o Debugging: Debugging scripts can be challenging. Use debugging tools and logging to identify and resolve issues.

By mastering AI perception, decision-making, and scripting, game developers can create intelligent and engaging AI agents that bring virtual worlds to life.

CHAPTER 12

Game Data Management and Serialization

Game Data Management and Serialization are essential for efficient game development.[1] Choosing appropriate data structures (XML, JSON, Binary) impacts performance and maintainability.[2] Serialization converts game data for storage/transmission, while deserialization reconstructs it. Effective asset management, including organization and loading, optimizes resource handling.[3] Database integration allows for persistent data storage (player profiles, game saves).[4] Mastering these areas ensures robust, scalable, and performant game systems.

12.1 Data Structures for Game Data (XML, JSON, Binary Formats)

Choosing the right data structure is crucial for efficient storage, retrieval, and manipulation of game data.

- XML (Extensible Markup Language):
  - Overview:
    - XML is a markup language that defines a set of rules for encoding documents in a format that is both human-readable and machine-readable.[2]
    - It uses tags to define[3] elements and attributes, creating a hierarchical data structure.[4]
  - Features:
    - Human-readable and editable.
    - Platform-independent.[5]

- Supports complex data structures.[6]
- Widely used for configuration files and data exchange.[7]
- Advantages:
  - Highly flexible and extensible.[8]
  - Well-supported by parsers and libraries.
  - Self-describing data format.[9]
- Disadvantages:
  - Verbose and large file sizes.
  - Slower parsing compared to binary formats.
  - Can be complex for simple data.
- Use Cases:
  - Configuration files.
  - Level data.
  - Game settings.

- Data exchange between systems.
- JSON (JavaScript Object Notation):
  - Overview:
    - JSON is a lightweight data-interchange format that is easy for humans to read and write and easy for machines to parse and generate.[10]
    - It is based on a subset of[11] the JavaScript programming language.[1213]
    - It utilizes key-value pairs and arrays to represent data.[14]
  - Features:
    - Human-readable and lightweight.[15]
    - Platform-independent.
    - Easy to parse and generate.

- Widely used for web services and data exchange.[16]
- Advantages:
    - Compact and efficient.
    - Fast parsing and generation.
    - Simple and intuitive syntax.
    - Excellent for web related tasks.
- Disadvantages:
    - Less flexible than XML for complex data structures.
    - No support for comments.
    - Lack of schema support natively.
- Use Cases:
    - Web services and APIs.
    - Configuration files.
    - Game state data.
    - Data storage.
- Binary Formats:
    - Overview:

- Binary formats store data in a raw, machine-readable format.[17]
- They are typically more compact and faster to parse than text-based formats.

- Features:
  - Compact file sizes.
  - Fast parsing and generation.
  - Direct memory mapping.
  - Customizable for specific game data.
- Advantages:
  - High performance.
  - Minimal storage overhead.
  - Direct control over data layout.
- Disadvantages:
  - Not human-readable.
  - Platform-dependent.

- - Requires custom parsers and generators.
  - Harder to debug.
  - Use Cases:
    - Game assets (textures, meshes, audio).[18]
    - Large game state data.
    - Performance-critical applications.
    - Networking data.
- Choosing a Data Format:
  - Data Complexity: Consider the complexity of the game data.
  - Performance Requirements: Evaluate the performance requirements of loading and saving data.
  - Human Readability: Determine if human readability is essential.
  - Platform Compatibility: Ensure that the chosen format is compatible with the target platforms.

- ○ Development Tools: Consider the availability of parsers and libraries for the chosen format.

12.2 Serialization and Deserialization: Loading and Saving Game Data

Serialization and deserialization are essential processes for loading and saving game data.

- Serialization:
  - ○ Definition: Serialization is the process of converting game data into a format that can be stored or transmitted.[19]
  - ○ Techniques:
    - Converting game objects and data structures into XML, JSON, or binary representations.
    - Writing serialized data to files or network streams.

- - Using libraries and frameworks to automate the serialization process.
  - Considerations:
    - Data versioning to handle changes in data structures.
    - Data compression to reduce file sizes.
    - Data encryption to protect sensitive data.
- Deserialization:
  - Definition: Deserialization is the process of converting serialized data back into game objects and data structures.
  - Techniques:
    - Parsing serialized data from files or network streams.
    - Creating game objects and data structures based on the parsed data.

- Using libraries and frameworks to automate the deserialization process.
- Considerations:
    - Error handling to handle invalid or corrupted data.
    - Memory management to avoid memory leaks.
    - Performance optimization to minimize loading times.
- Serialization Libraries and Frameworks:
    - Boost.Serialization: A C++ library for serializing and deserializing objects.[20]
    - Google Protocol Buffers: A language-neutral, platform-neutral, extensible mechanism for serializing structured data.[21]
    - JSON libraries: RapidJSON, nlohmann/json.
    - XML libraries: TinyXML-2, pugixml.

- Data Versioning:
  - Importance: Game data structures can change over time.[22] Data versioning ensures compatibility between different versions of the game.
  - Techniques:
    - Storing a version number in the serialized data.
    - Implementing migration scripts to convert data between versions.
    - Using schema evolution techniques.
- Data Compression:
  - Importance: Data compression reduces file sizes, improving loading times and reducing storage requirements.[23]
  - Techniques:
    - Using compression algorithms like zlib or LZ4.
    - Compressing specific data sections or entire files.

- Data Encryption:
  - Importance: Data encryption protects sensitive game data from unauthorized access.[24]
  - Techniques:
    - Using encryption algorithms like AES or RSA.
    - Encrypting specific data sections or entire files.
- Considerations:
  - Performance: Optimize serialization and deserialization processes for performance.
  - Memory Usage: Manage memory efficiently to avoid memory leaks.
  - Error Handling: Implement robust error handling to handle invalid or corrupted data.
  - Security: Protect sensitive game data from unauthorized access.

- Maintainability: Design data management systems that are easy to understand and modify.

By mastering game data management and serialization, game developers can create robust, efficient, and maintainable data systems that enhance the overall game development process.

12.3 Asset Management: Organizing and Loading Game Resources

Efficient asset management is vital for maintaining a streamlined development pipeline and ensuring optimal game performance.

- **Asset Organization:**
  - **Hierarchical Structure:**
    - Organize assets in a hierarchical folder structure that mirrors the game's structure.[1]

- Use descriptive folder names to facilitate asset location.[2]
- **Naming Conventions:**
  - Establish consistent naming conventions for assets to ensure uniformity and clarity.[3]
  - Use prefixes, suffixes, and categories to organize assets.[4]
- **Metadata Management:**
  - Store metadata for assets, such as author, creation date, and usage information.[5]
  - Use metadata to search, filter, and manage assets.[6]
- **Asset Bundling:**
  - Group related assets into asset bundles for efficient loading and management.[7]

- Asset bundles can be compressed and loaded asynchronously.[8]
  - **Version Control:**
    - Use version control systems (e.g., Git, Perforce) to track asset changes and collaborate effectively.[9]
    - Store binary assets using Large File Storage extensions when needed.[10]
- **Asset Loading:**
  - **Asynchronous Loading:**
    - Load assets asynchronously to prevent game stalls and improve loading times.
    - Use background threads or coroutines to load assets in the background.[11]
  - **Resource Caching:**
    - Implement resource caching to avoid reloading

assets that are already in memory.

- Use a least recently used (LRU) cache to manage the resource cache.

- **Streaming Assets:**
  - Stream large assets (e.g., textures, audio) from disk to reduce memory usage.[12]
  - Use streaming techniques to load assets on demand.[13]

- **Asset Compression:**
  - Compress assets to reduce file sizes and loading times.[14]
  - Use appropriate compression algorithms for different asset types.

- **Asset Pipelines:**
  - Create asset pipelines to automate asset processing and conversion.[15]

- Asset pipelines can handle tasks like texture compression, mesh optimization, and audio encoding.[16]
  - **Runtime Asset Bundling:**
    - Create or modify asset bundles at runtime.
- **Asset Management Tools:**
  - **Custom Asset Managers:**
    - Develop custom asset managers to handle specific game requirements.
    - Custom asset managers can provide features like asset versioning, dependency tracking, and runtime asset manipulation.
  - **Game Engine Asset Systems:**
    - Utilize the asset management systems

provided by game engines (e.g., Unity, Unreal Engine).[17]

- Game engine asset systems offer features like asset importing, organization, and loading.[18]

- **Considerations:**
  - **Performance:** Optimize asset loading and management for performance.
  - **Memory Usage:** Minimize memory usage by streaming and caching assets.
  - **Scalability:** Design asset management systems that can scale with the size of the game.[19]
  - **Maintainability:** Create asset management systems that are easy to understand and modify.

12.4　Database Integration: Storing Persistent Game Data

Database integration is essential for storing and managing persistent game data, such as player profiles, game saves, and online leaderboards.[20]

- **Database Types:**
  - **Relational Databases (SQL):**
    - Relational databases (e.g., MySQL, PostgreSQL, SQLite) store data in tables with predefined schemas.[21]
    - They are well-suited for structured data and complex queries.
  - **NoSQL Databases:**
    - NoSQL databases (e.g., MongoDB, Redis, Cassandra) store data in flexible formats, such as JSON or key-value pairs.[22]

- They are well-suited for unstructured or semi-structured data and high-performance applications.
  - **Embedded Databases:**
    - Embedded databases (e.g., SQLite, LevelDB) are lightweight databases that can be embedded directly into the game.[23]
    - They are well-suited for storing local game data.
- **Database Integration Techniques:**
  - **Database Drivers:**
    - Use database drivers to connect to and interact with databases from the game.
    - Database drivers provide APIs for executing SQL queries or NoSQL operations.[24]

- Object-Relational Mapping (ORM):
  - Use ORM libraries to map game objects to database tables.
  - ORM libraries simplify database access and reduce boilerplate code.[25]
- Data Access Objects (DAOs):
  - Create DAOs to encapsulate database access logic.
  - DAOs provide a clean and consistent interface for interacting with the database.[26]
- Asynchronous Database Operations:
  - Perform database operations asynchronously to prevent game stalls.

- Use background threads or coroutines to execute database queries.
- **Data Storage Considerations:**
  - **Player Profiles:** Store player profiles, including usernames, passwords, and game settings.
  - **Game Saves:** Store game save data, including player progress, inventory, and game state.
  - **Online Leaderboards:** Store player scores and leaderboard data.
  - **Game Statistics:** Store game statistics, such as player achievements and playtime.
  - **In-Game Purchases:** Store information about in-game purchases and virtual items.[27]
- **Database Security:**
  - **Data Encryption:** Encrypt sensitive data, such as passwords and personal information.[28]

- **Access Control:** Implement access control mechanisms to restrict database access.[29]
- **SQL Injection Prevention:** Sanitize user input to prevent SQL injection attacks.[30]
- **Database Firewalls:** Use database firewalls to protect the database from unauthorized access.

- **Database Optimization:**
  - **Indexing:** Use indexes to improve query performance.
  - **Query Optimization:** Optimize SQL queries for efficiency.
  - **Connection Pooling:** Use connection pooling to reduce database connection overhead.[31]
  - **Data Caching:** Cache frequently accessed data to reduce database load.
- **Considerations:**

- ○ **Scalability:** Choose a database that can scale with the number of players and game data.
- ○ **Performance:** Optimize database queries and data access for performance.
- ○ **Security:** Implement robust security measures to protect game data.
- ○ **Maintainability:** Design database schemas and data access logic that are easy to understand and modify.

By mastering asset management and database integration, game developers can create robust, scalable, and maintainable game systems that enhance the overall game development process and player experience.

CHAPTER 13

Optimization and Performance Tuning

Optimization and performance tuning are crucial for delivering smooth, responsive gameplay.[1] This involves profiling to identify bottlenecks (CPU, GPU, memory), followed by targeted optimizations.[2] Techniques include memory reduction (object pooling, texture compression), CPU improvements (vectorization, multithreading), and GPU enhancements (minimizing draw calls, simplifying shaders). Effective optimization ensures a stable frame rate and efficient resource usage, leading to a better player experience.[3]

13.1 Profiling and Performance Analysis: Identifying Bottlenecks

Profiling and performance analysis are essential for identifying performance bottlenecks and optimizing game code.[1]

- Profiling Tools:
  - CPU Profilers:
    - Tools that measure CPU usage and identify performance hotspots.[2]
    - Examples: Intel VTune, AMD μProf, Instruments (macOS), Perf (Linux).[3]
  - GPU Profilers:
    - Tools that measure GPU usage and identify rendering bottlenecks.[4]
    - Examples: RenderDoc, NVIDIA Nsight, AMD Radeon GPU Profiler.[5]
  - Memory Profilers:
    - Tools that track memory allocation and identify memory leaks.[6]

- Examples: Valgrind, AddressSanitizer, Memory Profiler (Unity).[7]
  - Frame Profilers:
    - Tools that analyze frame rendering performance and identify bottlenecks.[8]
    - Examples: Built-in profilers in game engines (Unity, Unreal Engine).[9]
  - Custom Profilers:
    - Implement custom profilers to measure specific game systems or algorithms.
    - Use timers and counters to track performance metrics.
- Performance Analysis Techniques:
  - Hotspot Analysis:
    - Identify functions or code sections that consume the most CPU or GPU time.
    - Focus optimization efforts on these hotspots.

- Call Graph Analysis:
  - Analyze the call graph to identify performance bottlenecks in function calls.
  - Optimize function calls and reduce function call overhead.
- Memory Leak Detection:
  - Use memory profilers to detect memory leaks and prevent memory exhaustion.[10]
  - Fix memory leaks to improve game stability and performance.
- Frame Rate Analysis:
  - Analyze frame rate fluctuations and identify causes of frame drops.
  - Optimize rendering and game logic to maintain a stable frame rate.
- Benchmarking:

- - Measure the performance of specific game systems or algorithms using benchmarks.
  - Compare performance results before and after optimization.
- Identifying Bottlenecks:
  - CPU-Bound Bottlenecks:
    - Occur when the CPU is the limiting factor in performance.
    - Symptoms: High CPU usage, low frame rate.
  - GPU-Bound Bottlenecks:
    - Occur when the GPU is the limiting factor in performance.
    - Symptoms: Low frame rate, high GPU usage, low CPU usage.
  - Memory-Bound Bottlenecks:
    - Occur when memory access or allocation is the

limiting factor in performance.

- Symptoms: High memory usage, frequent garbage collection, memory leaks.
  - I/O-Bound Bottlenecks:
    - Occur when disk or network I/O is the limiting factor in performance.
    - Symptoms: Long loading times, network latency.
- Considerations:
  - Real-Time Profiling: Profile game performance in real-time to identify dynamic bottlenecks.
  - Representative Scenes: Profile game performance in representative scenes or levels.
  - Target Platforms: Profile game performance on target platforms to identify platform-specific bottlenecks.[11]

○ Profiling Overhead: Be aware of the overhead introduced by profiling tools.

13.2 Memory Optimization Techniques: Reducing Memory Footprint

Reducing memory footprint is crucial for improving game performance and stability, especially on platforms with limited memory.[12]

- Memory Allocation Strategies:
  - ○ Object Pooling:
    - ■ Reuse objects instead of allocating and deallocating them frequently.
    - ■ Object pooling reduces memory fragmentation and improves performance.[13]
  - ○ Arena Allocation:

- Allocate memory in large chunks and manage it manually.
- Arena allocation reduces memory fragmentation and improves allocation speed.[14]
  - Stack Allocation:
    - Allocate memory on the stack for temporary variables and data structures.
    - Stack allocation is faster than heap allocation.
- Data Structure Optimization:
  - Use Efficient Data Structures:
    - Choose data structures that minimize memory usage and provide efficient access.
    - Examples: Use arrays instead of linked lists for sequential data, use hash tables for fast lookups.

- Data Compression:
  - Compress data to reduce memory usage.
  - Use appropriate compression algorithms for different data types.
- Data Alignment:
  - Align data structures to improve memory access performance.
  - Align data structures to cache line boundaries.
- Texture Optimization:
  - Texture Compression:
    - Use texture compression formats (e.g., S3TC, ASTC) to reduce texture memory usage.[15]
    - Choose appropriate compression formats for different texture types.
  - Mipmapping:
    - Use mipmaps to reduce texture aliasing and

improve rendering performance.[16]
- Mipmaps reduce texture memory usage for distant objects.
- Texture Atlases:
  - Combine multiple textures into a single texture atlas to reduce draw calls and memory usage.
  - Texture atlases improve rendering performance and reduce memory usage.[17]
- Mesh Optimization:
  - Vertex Compression:
    - Compress vertex data to reduce mesh memory usage.
    - Use appropriate compression techniques for different vertex attributes.
  - Index Buffer Optimization:

- Optimize index buffers to reduce mesh memory usage.
- Use 16-bit indices when possible.
  - Level of Detail (LOD):
    - Use LOD techniques to render meshes with varying levels of detail based on their distance from the camera.
    - LOD reduces mesh memory usage and improves rendering performance.[18]
- Audio Optimization:
  - Audio Compression:
    - Use audio compression formats (e.g., Ogg Vorbis, MP3) to reduce audio memory usage.
    - Choose appropriate compression formats for different audio types.

- Audio Streaming:
  - Stream large audio files from disk to reduce memory usage.
  - Audio streaming reduces memory usage and improves loading times.[19]
- Considerations:
  - Platform Memory Limits: Consider the memory limits of target platforms.
  - Memory Fragmentation: Minimize memory fragmentation to improve memory allocation performance.
  - Garbage Collection: Minimize garbage collection overhead to improve performance.[20]

13.3 CPU Optimization: Vectorization and Multithreading

CPU optimization techniques like vectorization and multithreading can significantly improve game performance.

- Vectorization (SIMD):
  - Concept:
    - Vectorization involves performing the same operation on multiple data elements simultaneously using SIMD (Single Instruction, Multiple Data) instructions.[21]
    - SIMD instructions can significantly improve performance for data-parallel tasks.[22]
  - Techniques:
    - Use compiler intrinsics or SIMD libraries (e.g., Intel

AVX, ARM NEON) to write vectorized code.
  - Align data structures to vector register boundaries.
  - Optimize loops for vectorization.
  - Use Cases:
    - Physics simulations, particle systems, image processing.
- Multithreading:
  - Concept:
    - Multithreading involves dividing tasks into multiple threads that run concurrently on different CPU cores.[23]
    - Multithreading can significantly improve performance for parallel tasks.[24]
  - Techniques:
    - Use thread pools to manage threads efficiently.

- Use synchronization primitives (e.g., mutexes, semaphores) to prevent race conditions.[25]
- Optimize data structures for concurrent access.
  - Use Cases:
    - Physics simulations, AI, rendering, asset loading.
- Task Parallelism:
  - Divide tasks into independent subtasks that can be executed concurrently.
  - Use task-based parallelism libraries (e.g., Intel TBB, C++17 std::async).[26]
- Data Parallelism:
  - Perform the same operation on multiple data elements concurrently.
  - Use vectorization or multithreading for data-parallel tasks.
- Considerations:

- Thread Safety: Ensure that data structures and functions are thread-safe.
- Synchronization Overhead: Minimize synchronization overhead to avoid performance bottlenecks.
- Load Balancing: Distribute tasks evenly across threads to maximize CPU utilization.

13.4 GPU Optimization: Minimizing Draw Calls and Shader Complexity

GPU optimization techniques can significantly improve rendering performance.[27]

- Minimizing Draw Calls:
    - Batching:
        - Combine multiple draw calls into a single draw call.

- Use techniques like static batching and dynamic batching.
- Instancing:
  - Render multiple instances of the same mesh with different transformations and materials.
  - Instancing reduces draw calls and improves rendering performance.[28]
- Texture Atlases:
  - Combine multiple textures into a single texture atlas to reduce draw calls.
  - Texture atlases improve rendering performance and reduce memory usage.[29]
- Geometry Shaders:
  - Geometry shaders can be used to generate geometry on the GPU, reducing the number of draw calls.

- Shader Complexity:
  - Simplify Shaders:
    - Reduce the complexity of shaders to improve rendering performance.
    - Minimize the number of arithmetic operations and texture lookups.
  - Use Low-Precision Data:
    - Use low-precision floating-point types (e.g., half-precision) when possible.
    - Low-precision data reduces memory usage and improves rendering performance.[30]
  - Optimize Texture Sampling:
    - Use texture filtering and mipmapping to improve texture quality.
    - Use texture compression to reduce texture memory usage.

- Avoid Branching:
    - Minimize the use of conditional statements in shaders.
    - Branching can cause performance bottlenecks.[31]
- Overdraw Reduction:
    - Depth Testing:
        - Use depth testing to prevent rendering pixels that are hidden behind other objects.
        - Depth testing reduces overdraw and improves rendering performance.
    - Frustum Culling:
        - Cull objects that are outside the camera's view frustum.
        - Frustum culling reduces the number of objects rendered.[32]
    - Occlusion Culling:

- - Cull objects that are hidden behind other objects.
  - Occlusion culling reduces the number of pixels rendered.[33]
- GPU Instancing and Mesh Shaders:
  - GPU Instancing: Render many copies of the same mesh with different parameters.
  - Mesh Shaders: Allow for more control over vertex processing and geometry generation.[34]
- Considerations:
  - GPU Architecture: Consider the architecture of target GPUs when optimizing shaders.
  - Rendering Pipeline: Optimize the rendering pipeline for performance.
  - Draw Call Analysis: Use GPU profilers to analyze draw call performance.

By mastering these optimization and performance tuning techniques, game developers can create smooth, responsive, and visually stunning games that deliver immersive gameplay experiences.

CHAPTER 14

Cross-Platform Development and Deployment

Cross-platform game development aims to reach a wider audience by building games for PC, consoles, and mobile.[1] Utilizing game engines like Unity and Unreal Engine, along with libraries like SDL and GLFW, simplifies this process.[2] Platform-specific optimizations are crucial for performance.[3]

Deployment involves navigating the unique requirements of each platform, from PC distribution on Steam to console certification and mobile app stores.[4] Effective packaging, marketing, and post-launch support are essential for a successful cross-platform release.

14.1 Building Games for PC, Console, and Mobile Platforms

Developing games for a variety of platforms requires a comprehensive understanding of their unique characteristics and limitations.

- PC Platform:
  - Hardware Diversity:
    - PCs have a wide range of hardware configurations, from low-end laptops to high-end gaming rigs.
    - Game developers must consider scalability and performance across this diverse hardware landscape.[1]
  - Operating Systems:
    - Windows, macOS, and Linux are the primary operating systems.[2]
    - Cross-platform frameworks and libraries are essential for

supporting multiple operating systems.[3]

- Input Devices:
  - Keyboard, mouse, and gamepads are common input devices.[4]
  - Game developers must support multiple input devices and provide customizable input mappings.
- Distribution:
  - Digital distribution platforms (e.g., Steam, Epic Games Store, GOG) are the primary channels for PC game distribution.[5]
  - Consider DRM (Digital Rights Management) and online services integration.
- Considerations:
  - Graphics API selection (DirectX, Vulkan, OpenGL).

- - Driver compatibility and updates.
  - User interface design for varied screen resolutions.
- Console Platforms:
  - Hardware Consistency:
    - Consoles have standardized hardware configurations, simplifying optimization and development.[6]
    - However, each console platform has its own unique hardware and software architecture.
  - Platform-Specific SDKs:
    - Console development requires using platform-specific SDKs (Software Development Kits) provided by console manufacturers.

- These SDKs provide access to console hardware and APIs.
- Certification and Submission:
  - Console game releases require certification and submission processes to ensure compliance with platform requirements.[7]
  - These processes can be lengthy and require meticulous attention to detail.
- Input Devices:
  - Console gamepads are the primary input devices.[8]
  - Game developers must design intuitive and responsive controls for gamepads.
- Distribution:
  - Digital and physical distribution through

console online stores and retail channels.[9]

- Considerations:
  - Memory limitations and optimization.
  - Specific console features (e.g., haptic feedback, motion controls).
  - Adherence to platform-specific guidelines.

- Mobile Platforms:
  - Hardware Limitations:
    - Mobile devices have limited processing power, memory, and battery life.[10]
    - Game developers must optimize performance and minimize resource usage.[11]
  - Operating Systems:
    - Android and iOS are the dominant mobile operating systems.[12]

- Cross-platform frameworks are essential for supporting both operating systems.
- Input Devices:
  - Touchscreens are the primary input devices.
  - Game developers must design intuitive and responsive touch controls.
- Distribution:
  - App stores (e.g., Google Play Store, Apple App Store) are the primary channels for mobile game distribution.[13]
  - Consider in-app purchases and advertising models.
- Considerations:
  - Battery consumption and thermal management.
  - Screen size and aspect ratio variations.

- Network connectivity and data usage.
- Touch screen interface design.
- Cross-Platform Development Tools:
    - Game Engines:
        - Unity and Unreal Engine are popular cross-platform game engines that simplify development for multiple platforms.[14]
        - These engines provide tools for asset management, rendering, and platform-specific builds.[15]
    - Cross-Platform Libraries:
        - SDL (Simple DirectMedia Layer) and other cross-platform libraries provide abstractions for graphics, input, and audio.[16]

- These libraries simplify platform-specific code.
  - Scripting Languages:
    - Scripting languages like Lua and Python can be used to write platform-independent game logic.[17]
    - Scripting languages enhance portability and maintainability.

14.2 Platform-Specific Considerations and Optimizations

Each platform has unique characteristics that require specific considerations and optimizations.

- PC Optimizations:
  - Graphics Settings:
    - Provide customizable graphics settings to

accommodate a wide range of hardware.

- Implement adaptive graphics settings to adjust quality based on hardware performance.
  - Input Mapping:
    - Allow players to customize input mappings for keyboard, mouse, and gamepads.
    - Provide default input mappings for common input devices.
  - Performance Profiling:
    - Use performance profiling tools to identify bottlenecks on different hardware configurations.
    - Optimize code and assets for specific hardware.
- Console Optimizations:
  - Memory Management:

- Optimize memory usage to stay within console memory limitations.
- Use memory profiling tools to identify and fix memory leaks.
  - Thread Optimization:
    - Utilize console multi-core CPUs effectively by implementing multithreaded code.
    - Optimize thread synchronization to minimize overhead.
  - GPU Optimizations:
    - Optimize shaders and rendering pipelines for console GPUs.
    - Minimize draw calls and overdraw.
- Mobile Optimizations:
  - Battery Optimization:
    - Minimize battery consumption by

optimizing CPU and GPU usage.
- Implement power-saving modes and reduce frame rates when appropriate.
  - Memory Optimization:
    - Optimize memory usage to stay within mobile device memory limitations.
    - Use texture compression and asset streaming to reduce memory footprint.
  - Touch Input Optimization:
    - Design intuitive and responsive touch controls.
    - Optimize touch input handling for performance.
  - Network Optimization:
    - Minimize network data usage.
    - Optimize network traffic.
- Cross-Platform Optimization:
  - Conditional Compilation:

- - Use conditional compilation to include or exclude platform-specific code.
  - This allows for platform-specific optimizations without duplicating code.
  - Abstraction Layers:
    - Create abstraction layers for platform-specific APIs.
    - This simplifies platform-specific code and improves portability.
  - Data-Driven Design:
    - Use data-driven design to separate game logic from platform-specific code.
    - This allows for easier porting and maintenance.
- Testing:
  - Thorough testing on all target platforms is essential.

○ Automated testing, and manual testing, are both very important.

By understanding the unique characteristics of each platform and implementing appropriate optimizations, game developers can create high-quality games that reach a wider audience.

14.3   Using   Cross-Platform Libraries and Frameworks

Cross-platform libraries and frameworks are the linchpins of modern game development, enabling developers to write code once and deploy it across multiple platforms.[1]

- Game Engines:
  - Unity:
    - Overview: A versatile and user-friendly engine supporting a wide range of platforms, from mobile to consoles and PC.[2]
    - Features: Visual editor, asset pipeline, scripting (C#), extensive plugin

ecosystem, multi-platform build support.[3]

- Educational Value: Unity provides a comprehensive introduction to game development concepts and cross-platform workflows.
- Unreal Engine:
    - Overview: A powerful engine known for its high-fidelity graphics and advanced features.[4]
    - Features: Blueprint visual scripting, C++ support, advanced rendering capabilities, robust networking, multi-platform build support.[5]
    - Educational Value: Unreal Engine delves into advanced rendering techniques and C++ game development.[6]

- Godot Engine:
  - Overview: A free and open-source engine with a focus on 2D and 3D game development.[7]
  - Features: GDScript (Python-like scripting), visual editor, node-based architecture, multi-platform build support.[8]
  - Educational Value: Godot emphasizes open-source development and provides a flexible and accessible engine.[9]
- Cross-Platform Libraries:
  - SDL (Simple DirectMedia Layer):
    - Overview: A cross-platform development library providing low-level access to audio, keyboard, mouse,

joystick, and graphics hardware.[10]

- Features: Platform-independent API, support for OpenGL/Vulkan, audio mixing, input handling.
- Educational Value: SDL provides a foundational understanding of low-level system interactions.[11]

○ GLFW (Graphics Library Framework):[12]

- Overview: A lightweight, cross-platform library for window management, OpenGL context creation, and input handling.[13]
- Features: Window creation, OpenGL context management, input handling, cross-platform compatibility.

- Educational Value: GLFW focuses on graphics programming and provides a simple interface for OpenGL development.[14]
  -
  - Qt:
    - Overview: A cross-platform application framework with extensive UI and multimedia capabilities.
    - Features: UI design tools, networking, database access, multimedia support, cross-platform compatibility.
    - Educational Value: Qt demonstrates the power of a comprehensive application framework and its application in game tools.[15]

- Boost.Asio:
  - Overview: A cross-platform C++ library for network and low-level I/O programming.[16]
  - Features: Asynchronous I/O, TCP/UDP sockets, timers, cross-platform compatibility.
  - Educational Value: Boost.Asio teaches advanced network programming concepts and asynchronous I/O techniques.[17]
- Scripting Languages:
  - Lua:
    - Overview: A lightweight and fast scripting language often used for game logic and AI.[18]
    - Features: Simple syntax, embeddable, efficient execution.

- - **Educational Value:** Lua demonstrates the benefits of scripting languages for rapid prototyping and dynamic game logic.[19]
  - Python:
    - **Overview:** A versatile and powerful scripting language with extensive libraries.
    - **Features:** Readability, extensive libraries, rapid development.
    - **Educational Value:** Python introduces a powerful scripting language applicable to various game development tasks.[20]
- Choosing the Right Tools:
  - Project Requirements: Consider the game's genre, complexity, and target platforms.

- Team Expertise: Evaluate the team's familiarity with different tools and technologies.
- Performance Requirements: Choose tools that meet the game's performance requirements.
- Development Speed: Consider the development speed and ease of use of different tools.
- Community Support: Evaluate the community support and availability of resources for different tools.

14.4 Packaging and Distribution: Deploying Your Game

Packaging and distribution are the final steps in the game development process, bringing your game to the players.

- PC Distribution:
  - Digital Distribution Platforms:
    - Steam: The dominant digital distribution

platform for PC games, offering a wide audience and community features.[21]

- Epic Games Store: A digital storefront with a focus on developer revenue sharing and exclusive titles.[22]
- GOG (Good Old Games): A platform specializing in DRM-free games.
- Itch.io: A platform for indie developers to distribute their games.[23]

o Packaging:

- Create installers or archives for different operating systems (Windows, macOS, Linux).
- Consider using installation tools like Inno Setup or NSIS.
- Implement auto-update mechanisms.

- ○ DRM (Digital Rights Management):
    - ■ Consider using DRM to protect your game from piracy.
    - ■ Balance DRM effectiveness with user experience.
- Console Distribution:
    - ○ Platform-Specific Submission Processes:
        - ■ Follow the certification and submission guidelines provided by console manufacturers (Sony, Microsoft, Nintendo).
        - ■ These processes involve rigorous testing and compliance checks.
    - ○ Digital and Physical Distribution:
        - ■ Distribute your game through console online stores (PlayStation Store,

Xbox Store, Nintendo eShop).
- Consider physical distribution through retail channels.
  - Platform-Specific Requirements:
    - Adhere to platform-specific technical requirements and guidelines.
    - Optimize your game for console hardware.
- Mobile Distribution:
  - App Stores:
    - Google Play Store: The primary distribution platform for Android games.[24]
    - Apple App Store: The primary distribution platform for iOS games.
  - Packaging:

- - Create APK (Android) or IPA (iOS) packages for distribution.
  - Consider using app bundling and asset delivery networks.
  - In-App Purchases and Advertising:
    - Implement in-app purchases and advertising models to monetize your game.
    - Adhere to app store guidelines for in-app purchases and advertising.[25]
  - Localization:
    - Localize your game for different languages and regions.
    - Consider cultural differences and regional preferences.
- Cross-Platform Distribution:

- Cloud Gaming Platforms:
    - Consider distributing your game through cloud gaming platforms (e.g., Google Stadia, NVIDIA GeForce Now).
    - Cloud gaming platforms offer cross-platform play without requiring local installations.[26]
- Web-Based Distribution:
    - Distribute your game through web browsers using technologies like WebGL.[27]
    - Web-based distribution offers cross-platform play without requiring downloads.
- Marketing and Promotion:
    - Build a Community: Engage with players through social media, forums, and Discord.

- Create a Trailer: Showcase your game's features and gameplay in a compelling trailer.
- Reach Out to Influencers: Collaborate with streamers and YouTubers to promote your game.[28]
- Participate in Events: Attend game conventions and events to showcase your game.
- Run Ad Campaigns: Use online advertising platforms to reach potential players.
- Post-Launch Support:
  - Bug Fixes and Patches: Provide regular bug fixes and patches to improve the game.
  - Content Updates: Release new content updates to keep players engaged.
  - Community Engagement: Respond to player feedback and build a strong community.

By mastering the use of cross-platform tools and navigating the complexities of game packaging and distribution, developers can bring their games to a global audience, creating engaging experiences for players across multiple platforms.

CHAPTER 15

Debugging, Testing, and Quality Assurance

Debugging, testing, and quality assurance are vital for creating stable and enjoyable games.[1] Debugging involves using tools like debuggers and profilers to identify and fix errors and performance bottlenecks.[2] Unit and integration testing ensure code functionality and interaction.[3] Game testing and playtesting gather crucial player feedback.[4] Version control and collaboration tools facilitate team management and code integrity.[5] Automation and clear documentation streamline these processes, resulting in higher-quality game releases.[6]

15.1 Debugging Techniques: Using Debuggers and Profilers

Debugging is the art of identifying and resolving errors that hinder a game's functionality and performance.

- Debuggers: The Code Detectives
  - Overview: Debuggers are software tools that allow developers to step through code execution, inspect variables, and identify errors.
  - Techniques:
    - Breakpoints: Setting breakpoints to pause execution at specific lines of code.
    - Step-Through Execution: Stepping through code line by line to trace execution flow.
    - Variable Inspection: Inspecting variable values to identify unexpected data.

- Watch Expressions: Monitoring variable values or expressions during execution.
- Call Stack Analysis: Tracing function calls to identify the source of errors.
  - Tools:
    - GDB (GNU Debugger): A powerful debugger for C/C++ development.
    - LLDB (Low Level Debugger): The default debugger on macOS and iOS.
    - Visual Studio Debugger: Integrated debugger for C# and C++ development in Visual Studio.
    - IDE Debuggers: Debuggers integrated into game engine IDEs (Unity, Unreal Engine).

- ○ Educational Value: Debuggers teach critical thinking and problem-solving skills, essential for all software development.
- Profilers: The Performance Analysts
  - ○ Overview: Profilers are tools that measure the performance of a game, identifying bottlenecks and areas for optimization.
  - ○ Techniques:
    - CPU Profiling: Measuring CPU usage to identify performance hotspots.
    - GPU Profiling: Measuring GPU usage to identify rendering bottlenecks.
    - Memory Profiling: Tracking memory allocation and identifying memory leaks.
    - Frame Profiling: Analyzing frame rendering performance to identify frame drops.

- Tools:
  - Intel VTune: A powerful CPU and GPU profiler.
  - AMD µProf: A CPU and GPU profiler for AMD platforms.
  - RenderDoc: A GPU profiler for analyzing rendering performance.
  - Valgrind: A memory profiler for detecting memory leaks.
  - Built-in Game Engine Profilers: Profilers integrated into game engines (Unity, Unreal Engine).
- Educational Value: Profilers demonstrate the importance of performance optimization and the impact of code choices on game performance.

15.2 Unit Testing and Integration Testing: Ensuring Code Quality

Testing is the process of verifying that a game's code functions correctly and meets quality standards.

- Unit Testing: Testing Individual Components
  - Overview: Unit testing involves testing individual functions or classes in isolation to ensure they function as expected.
  - Techniques:
    - Writing test cases that cover different input values and scenarios.
    - Using test frameworks to automate test execution and reporting.
    - Implementing test-driven development (TDD) to write tests before writing code.
  - Tools:

- Google Test: A C++ testing framework.
      - NUnit: A C# testing framework.
      - JUnit: A Java testing framework.
    - Educational Value: Unit testing emphasizes code correctness and maintainability, promoting good programming practices.
- Integration Testing: Testing Interacting Components
    - Overview: Integration testing involves testing the interactions between different components of a game to ensure they work together correctly.
    - Techniques:
      - Writing test cases that simulate realistic game scenarios.
      - Using test doubles (mocks, stubs) to isolate

components during testing.

- Implementing continuous integration (CI) to automate testing and deployment.
- Tools:
  - Selenium: A web testing framework that can be used for game UI testing.
  - Appium: A mobile testing framework.
  - Custom testing tools built into game engines.
- Educational Value: Integration testing highlights the importance of system-level testing and the challenges of complex interactions.

15.3 Game Testing and Playtesting: Gathering Feedback

Game testing and playtesting involve evaluating a game's gameplay, usability, and overall experience.

- Game Testing: Functionality and Stability
  - Overview: Game testing focuses on verifying that a game's features function correctly and that the game is stable.
  - Techniques:
    - Writing test cases that cover all game features and scenarios.
    - Performing regression testing to ensure that bug fixes do not introduce new issues.
    - Using automated testing tools to automate repetitive testing tasks.
  - Tools:

- TestRail, Zephyr, and other test case management tools.
- Game engine recording and playback tools.
  - Educational Value: Game testing demonstrates the importance of thorough testing and the challenges of complex game systems.
- Playtesting: User Experience and Gameplay
  - Overview: Playtesting involves gathering feedback from players to evaluate a game's gameplay, usability, and overall experience.
  - Techniques:
    - Conducting playtests with target audience members.
    - Observing player behavior and gathering feedback through surveys and interviews.

- Iterating on game design based on playtest feedback.
  - Educational Value: Playtesting emphasizes user-centered design and the importance of player feedback.

15.4 Version Control and Collaboration: Managing Development Teams

Version control and collaboration tools are essential for managing development teams and ensuring code integrity.

- Version Control: Tracking Code Changes
  - Overview: Version control systems track changes to code and other files, allowing developers to revert to previous versions and collaborate effectively.
  - Tools:

- Git: A distributed version control system widely used in game development.
- Perforce: A centralized version control system used by many AAA game studios.
- SVN (Subversion): A centralized version control system.
  - Educational Value: Version control teaches the importance of code management and collaboration in software development.
- Collaboration Tools: Facilitating Teamwork
  - Overview: Collaboration tools provide features for communication, task management, and code review.
  - Tools:

- Jira: A project management and issue tracking tool.
- Confluence: A team collaboration and documentation tool.
- Slack: A team communication platform.
- GitHub/GitLab: Platforms for code hosting, collaboration, and CI/CD.
  - Educational Value: Collaboration tools demonstrate the importance of teamwork and communication in software development.
- Continuous Integration (CI):
  - Overview: CI automates the process of building, testing, and deploying code changes.
  - Tools:
    - Jenkins, Travis CI, CircleCI, GitLab CI/CD, GitHub Actions.

○ Educational Value: CI emphasizes automation and efficiency in software development.

Post-Content Considerations:

- Automation: Automate as many testing and deployment processes as possible to improve efficiency and reduce errors.
- Documentation: Maintain clear and comprehensive documentation for code, testing procedures, and deployment processes.
- Communication: Foster open communication and collaboration between developers, testers, and other stakeholders.
- Iteration: Embrace an iterative development process, incorporating feedback from testing and playtesting to improve the game.
- Security: Integrate security testing into the development process to identify and address vulnerabilities.

By mastering debugging, testing, and quality assurance techniques, game developers can create high-quality games that provide enjoyable and engaging experiences for players.

Conclusion: The Future of C++ in Game Development

As we reach the culmination of our exploration into C++ game development, it's essential to reflect on the journey we've undertaken and peer into the horizon of this dynamic field. C++ has been, and continues to be, a cornerstone of game development, offering unparalleled performance and control.[1]

Summary of Key Concepts and Techniques

Throughout this journey, we've navigated the intricate landscape of C++ game development, covering a broad spectrum of critical concepts and techniques:

- Core C++ Fundamentals: We established a strong foundation in C++ programming, emphasizing object-oriented principles, memory management, and performance considerations.
- Graphics Programming: We delved into the world of graphics APIs (OpenGL, DirectX, Vulkan), exploring

shader programming (GLSL/HLSL), and mastering rendering techniques for both 2D and 3D environments.

- Game Physics and Collision Detection: We simulated realistic physics interactions and implemented collision detection algorithms, bringing virtual worlds to life.
- Audio Programming: We explored audio libraries and techniques for creating immersive soundscapes, enhancing the player's auditory experience.
- Networking and Multiplayer Development: We tackled the complexities of network protocols, client-server architecture, and state synchronization, enabling engaging multiplayer experiences.
- Game AI and Pathfinding: We crafted intelligent AI agents using state machines, behavior trees, and pathfinding algorithms, enriching gameplay with dynamic interactions.

- Game Data Management and Serialization: We mastered data structures and serialization techniques, ensuring efficient storage and retrieval of game data.
- Optimization and Performance Tuning: We honed our skills in profiling, memory optimization, CPU and GPU optimization, maximizing game performance.[2]
- Cross-Platform Development and Deployment: We navigated the intricacies of building and deploying games across diverse platforms, reaching a wider audience.
- Debugging, Testing, and Quality Assurance: We emphasized the importance of rigorous testing and debugging, ensuring game stability and quality.

These concepts and techniques form a powerful toolkit for any C++ game developer, enabling the creation of complex, high-performance games.

Emerging Trends and Technologies

The game development landscape is constantly evolving, with emerging trends and technologies shaping the future of C++ game development:

- Ray Tracing and Path Tracing: Real-time ray tracing and path tracing are revolutionizing graphics rendering, creating incredibly realistic lighting and reflections.[3] C++'s performance capabilities make it well-suited for implementing these demanding techniques.

- Machine Learning and AI: Machine learning is becoming increasingly integrated into game AI, enabling more intelligent and adaptive AI agents.[4] C++'s performance and control make it ideal for implementing machine learning algorithms.[5]

- Cloud Gaming and Streaming: Cloud gaming platforms are gaining popularity, allowing players to stream games without local installations.[6] C++'s cross-platform capabilities and performance make it suitable for developing cloud-based games.

- Virtual and Augmented Reality (VR/AR): VR and AR technologies are creating immersive and interactive experiences.[7] C++'s performance and low-level control are essential for developing VR/AR applications.[8]

- Procedural Generation: Procedural generation techniques are used to create dynamic and infinite game worlds.[9] C++'s performance and flexibility make it well-suited for implementing procedural generation algorithms.[10]

- Compute Shaders and GPGPU: General-purpose computing on GPUs (GPGPU) using compute shaders is becoming more common, enabling tasks like physics simulations, AI, and image processing. C++'s control over

GPU resources makes it ideal for GPGPU development.

- Modern C++ Standards: The continual evolution of the C++ standard, with features like coroutines, ranges, and modules, enhances productivity and performance.[11]

Continuing Your Learning Journey

The journey of a game developer is one of continuous learning and growth. Here are some avenues for continuing your learning journey:

- Advanced C++ Concepts: Delve deeper into advanced C++ topics like template metaprogramming, concurrency, and modern C++ features.
- Graphics Programming Mastery: Explore advanced graphics techniques like physically based rendering (PBR), global illumination, and ray tracing.

- Game Engine Development: Consider exploring game engine development to gain a deeper understanding of game architecture and implementation.
- Open-Source Contributions: Contribute to open-source game development projects to gain practical experience and collaborate with other developers.
- Game Jams and Competitions: Participate in game jams and competitions to challenge yourself and develop your skills.[12]
- Online Courses and Tutorials: Utilize online resources like Coursera, Udemy, and YouTube to learn new technologies and techniques.[13]
- Game Development Communities: Engage with game development communities on forums, Discord, and social media to learn from others and share your knowledge.

- Research Papers and Articles: Stay up-to-date with the latest research and advancements in game development.
- Experimentation and Practice: The most effective way to learn is by experimenting and practicing. Build your own projects and challenge yourself to create new and innovative games.

The future of C++ in game development is bright, with its performance, control, and flexibility making it an essential tool for creating the next generation of immersive and engaging games. By embracing emerging trends, continuing your learning journey, and honing your skills, you can contribute to the evolution of game development and create unforgettable gaming experiences.

Appendix: A Developer's Toolkit

This appendix provides a collection of essential resources, references, and troubleshooting guides to support your C++ game development endeavors.

A. C++ Standard Library Reference: Essential Classes and Functions

The C++ Standard Library is a treasure trove of tools for game development.[1] Mastering its essential components is paramount.

- Containers:
    - std::vector: Dynamically resizable arrays, crucial for managing game objects, particles, and dynamic data.
    - std::array: Fixed-size arrays, ideal for performance-critical data structures.
    - std::list: Doubly linked lists, useful for dynamic insertion and removal of elements.

- o std::map and std::unordered_map: Key-value pairs for efficient data lookups, essential for game settings, asset management, and AI.
- o std::set and std::unordered_set: Unique element collections, useful for managing unique IDs and flags.
- Algorithms:
  - o std::sort, std::find, std::transform, std::accumulate: Essential algorithms for data manipulation and processing.
  - o std::for_each, std::copy, std::move: Algorithms for efficient data iteration and transfer.
- Input/Output:
  - o std::fstream: File stream operations for loading and saving game data and assets.

- o std::stringstream: String stream operations for data formatting and parsing.
- Utilities:
  - o std::string: String manipulation and processing, essential for game text and UI.
  - o std::chrono: Time measurement and manipulation, crucial for game timing and animation.
  - o std::random: Random number generation, essential for game mechanics and procedural generation.
  - o std::thread and std::atomic: Threading and synchronization, crucial for multithreaded game development.
  - o std::variant and std::optional: Type-safe unions and optional values, improving code robustness.
- Memory Management:

- std::unique_ptr and std::shared_ptr: Smart pointers for automatic memory management, preventing memory leaks.

B. Common Game Development Libraries and Frameworks

Beyond the Standard Library, numerous libraries and frameworks enhance C++ game development.[2]

- Graphics Libraries:
  - OpenGL/Vulkan: Cross-platform graphics APIs for rendering 2D and 3D graphics.[3]
  - SDL (Simple DirectMedia Layer): A cross-platform library for graphics, audio, and input.
  - GLFW (Graphics Library Framework): A lightweight library for window management and OpenGL context creation.

- o Assimp (Open Asset Import Library): A library for importing 3D models and assets.
- Physics Engines:
  - o Box2D: A 2D physics engine for simulating rigid body dynamics.[4]
  - o Bullet Physics: A 3D physics engine for simulating rigid body and soft body dynamics.[5]
  - o PhysX: A powerful 3D physics engine with advanced features.
- Audio Libraries:
  - o FMOD: A powerful audio engine for creating immersive soundscapes.
  - o OpenAL: A cross-platform 3D audio API.
  - o SDL_mixer: An audio mixing library built on SDL.[6]
- Networking Libraries:
  - o Boost.Asio: A cross-platform library for network and low-level I/O programming.[7]

- ENet: A reliable UDP networking library for game development.[8]
- GUI Libraries:
  - Dear ImGui: An immediate mode GUI library for debugging and game tools.[9]
  - Qt: A cross-platform application framework with extensive UI capabilities.[10]

C. Performance Optimization Checklist

Optimizing game performance is crucial for smooth and immersive gameplay.

- Profiling:
  - Use CPU and GPU profilers to identify performance bottlenecks.
  - Measure frame rate and identify frame drops.
- Memory Optimization:
  - Use object pooling to reduce memory allocation overhead.
  - Compress textures and meshes to reduce memory footprint.

- Use smart pointers to manage memory automatically.
- CPU Optimization:
  - Use vectorization (SIMD) to perform parallel operations.
  - Implement multithreading to utilize multiple CPU cores.
  - Optimize algorithms and data structures for cache efficiency.
- GPU Optimization:
  - Minimize draw calls using batching and instancing.
  - Simplify shaders and reduce texture lookups.
  - Use level of detail (LOD) to render distant objects with lower detail.
  - Minimize overdraw using depth testing and culling.
- Asset Loading:
  - Load assets asynchronously to prevent game stalls.
  - Use asset streaming to load large assets on demand.

- o Implement resource caching to avoid reloading assets.

D. Glossary of Game Development Terms

A comprehensive glossary of common game development terms.

- AI (Artificial Intelligence): Simulating intelligent behavior in game agents.
- API (Application Programming Interface): A set of rules and specifications for interacting with software components.
- Asset: A game resource, such as a texture, model, audio file, or script.[11]
- Batching: Combining multiple draw calls into a single draw call.
- Collision Detection: Detecting when game objects collide.[12]
- Draw Call: A command sent to the GPU to render geometry.[13]
- Frame Rate: The number of frames rendered per second.
- GPU (Graphics Processing Unit): A specialized processor for rendering graphics.

- LOD (Level of Detail): Rendering objects with varying levels of detail based on distance.
- Mesh: A collection of vertices and triangles that define a 3D model.
- Shader: A program that runs on the GPU to process vertices and pixels.
- SIMD (Single Instruction, Multiple Data): Performing the same operation on multiple data elements simultaneously.[14]
- Texture: An image that is applied to a 3D model.
- Vertex: A point in 3D space that defines a mesh.[15]

E. Example Code Snippets and Project Setup Guides

Practical examples and setup guides for common game development tasks.

- OpenGL Project Setup: A guide to setting up an OpenGL project using GLFW and GLAD.

- Box2D Physics Integration: Example code for integrating Box2D into a game.
- Audio Playback with FMOD: Example code for playing audio using the FMOD library.
- Networking with Boost.Asio: Example code for implementing a simple client-server network.
- Shader Loading and Compilation: Example code for loading and compiling GLSL shaders.
- File I/O with fstream: Example code for loading and saving game data to a file.
- Threading example using std::thread: basic example of how to make a new thread.

F. Troubleshooting Common C++ Game Development Issues

A guide to troubleshooting common C++ game development issues.

- Memory Leaks: Using Valgrind to detect and fix memory leaks.[16]

- Rendering Errors: Debugging shader errors and OpenGL/Vulkan issues.
- Performance Bottlenecks: Identifying and resolving CPU and GPU bottlenecks.[17]
- Networking Issues: Troubleshooting network connectivity and latency problems.
- Build Errors: Resolving compiler and linker errors.
- Debugging Multithreaded Code: Using debuggers and synchronization techniques.

By providing these comprehensive resources, this appendix aims to empower developers to overcome challenges and create exceptional C++ games.